Who needs words?

Who needs words?

A Christian Communications Handbook

RICHARD LITTLEDALE

SAINT ANDREW PRESS
Edinburgh

First published in 2011 by
SAINT ANDREW PRESS
121 George Street
Edinburgh EH2 4YN

ISBN 978 0 7152 0943 1

British Library Cataloguing in Publication Data
A catalogue record for this book is available from the British Library

Typeset by Waverley Typesetters, Warham, Norfolk
Printed and bound by MPG Books, Bodmin

To Fiona – the bravest and best

Contents

Foreword

I grew up in Liverpool and belonged from infancy to a Baptist church there. I owe the church a great debt. It was there that I learned about the Christian faith, the importance of knowing why we believe what we think we believe, and the importance of belonging to a Christian community that combined generosity with community. But I also remember those years for another reason: a picture on the wall of one of the ancillary rooms.

Was Jesus a wimp in a white nightie, with blow-waves in his hair and a rather effete way of standing and pointing to young children? Was he really a pale Caucasian blond-haired man with beautifully manicured fingers and toes?

This isn't a critique of Victorian art; however, it does illustrate that communication is not something we 'do', but rather the 'pool we swim in' as conscious, self-referential human beings. Communication is going on all the time, in every encounter and every circumstance. My young mind was influenced by the pictures on the Sunday School walls, and the contradiction between what I saw and what I read in the Gospels became problematic for me. Jesus didn't get himself crucified for being 'nice'.

What this indicates is that the ability to communicate and be communicated with goes to the heart of what it is to be a human being living in society. And communication involves more than people talking to each other or trying to manipulate the minds and affections of potential consumers of goods. Communication is essentially about how we see the world, how we understand experience, how we relate to one another and to the context in which we are set. Communication is complex, intriguing and challenging. This makes it all the more concerning that so little attention is paid during our education to how communication works. It is perhaps as surprising as it is worrying that so many people whose work and purpose involve serious communication (preachers, politicians and so on) have obviously given so little thought to how they are doing what they are doing – and to how effective they are in doing it.

I remember sitting through a church service in the south of Germany and finding myself bemused by the inaccessibility of the sermon. The pastor seemed to be interested in his theme, but he seemed little concerned about whether we were as interested in it as he was. The content was not great, but it was the act of non-communication that intrigued me. After the service, he explained to me that people in that part of Germany are intelligent and, therefore, need a more intellectual sermon. I was too polite (or cowardly) to ask why it was, then, that the congregation seemed to be looking out of the windows at the heavily falling snow. If non-engagement of the congregation wasn't enough, then his lack of recognition of that non-engagement was even more worrying.

In theological terms, communication is at the beginning, middle and end of God's engagement with the world and his people. God speaks creation into being. His language is performative: it makes happen what it says. In the fourth Gospel, this is conveyed in the 'word' (Greek *logos*): 'In the beginning was the Word ...'. The first thing we know about God is that he communicates in a life-giving way: 'Let there be ...'. And it is not only 'word' but also 'light': God's creative nature and act both open up the world ('let there be') and illuminate it – contrary to the contemporary rumour about religious people which suggests that we are obsessed with closing down anything colourful and shutting out the light of anything we don't like.

According to the Biblical narrative, then, God's relationship with the creation is rooted in life-giving and illuminating communication. God speaks into being and then gives responsibility to his creation to be like him in communing and communicating within creation in a way that reflects his essential nature. One element of what is often called 'the fall' might be described as a human refusal to be creative, to illuminate, to communicate freely or to take responsibility for what we do with our freedom. Instead of 'letting be' – opening up potential for life-giving living – we exploit at the cost of our neighbours. Seen in this light, communication itself becomes a tool for protection or exploitation.

Language is amazing, and we too easily take for granted our human capacity for it. Linguistics is a minority interest, now threatened even further by a pragmatic political ideology that values only what is useful for producing 'wealth' as defined in financial or purely economic terms. The study of language demonstrates how language can be a means of opening up the imaginative worlds of ourselves and those with whom we communicate – but it can also be reduced to a narrow, self-protecting and defensive delineator of identity. In other words, instead of being a means of creatively expanding our understanding and experience of a world that is always bigger than our prejudices want to allow it to be, we use language as a barrier behind which a particular group (ethnic, social, ecclesial and so on) can hide.

There is an alternative. Go back to the Old Testament exiles of the sixth and eighth centuries before Christ, and we see more positively how language can work to challenge and open up a community. Consigned to exile, the people have to learn the language of what Walter Brueggemann calls 'the Empire'. They have to be able to live and work and function in the place of estrangement. They need to accept their situation, build their future and establish their families in a place that is not theirs. Furthermore, they have to come to terms with the fact that their being in the 'strange land' in the first place sets a huge question mark over their understanding of their identity and purpose in the world. (If their god is the creator of the cosmos, what are they doing now languishing by the banks of their oppressors' rivers, defeated by the tribal deities of the victors?)

Yet, into this experience of loss and deep self-questioning comes the haunting melody of a number of poets who see the circumstances of history through different eyes. They sing a song of 'home', a song that keeps alive the hope of a future – of renewed identity and of vindication – in such a way that their words tease a tired and cynical imagination, opening up a crack through which (as the great Leonard Cohen puts it) the light gets in. These poets have no patience with fantasy, self-justification or romantic nostalgia; they are realists and have no interest in their people escaping from facing responsibility for their own plight or being seduced or (in terms Karl Marx would recognise) sedated by some vague dream of 'heaven'. No, these poets (usually called 'prophets') live in the depths of the real world but know also that the future can be shaped by people who have vision and the courage to live into it – taking a long-term view of how history might develop into the future.

That is what makes these people powerful. They open up the future and do not collude with the miserable fantasy that all we need to do is knuckle down, hide our faces and wait for God to do something. That is why Jesus invited surprising people to live now as if a different world, with different rules, was already here; by doing so, this new world – or new way of living in the world – would be slowly shaped. It is world-affirming, future-opening and potential-shaping – a bit like the God of Genesis who speaks the creation into being.

All well and good. But what does this have to do with Richard Littledale's book on communication? Well, first, there is a need for a straightforward and simple book on communication that unpacks something of how communication works. There is plenty of material out there for people whose lives are taken up professionally (or academically) with the mechanics of communication, but there is little that can be taken up by ordinary people or those who need an accessible introduction to how communication can be thought about, developed and improved. This book does this. It will particularly help preachers, clergy and those involved in pastoral or communications work in and through the Christian churches. But it is not restricted to these. The author's concern is to think more generally about what makes for good communication. He has, therefore, written a book that will prove useful and constructive for anyone thinking through how communications work and can be improved in any particular community. As is obvious to anyone who thinks about it, communication always takes place in a particular context between particular agents and for particular purposes. There can be no ultimately disembodied communication – no general, airy-fairy stuff that can be thought about in the abstract. Therefore, thinking about what is going on in the communicative context of one particular community (in this case the Christian Church) can be constructively instructive for thinking about it in the context of another.

This book is thoughtful and practical. It is concerned with offering a first word on communication to people who haven't really thought too deeply about it before. It is, therefore, a first word and not the last. There are areas it does not address and matters it does not discuss. It does not attempt to explain for experts how their social-media engagement might be developed so that journalistic interconnectivity can be exploited for maximum effect in relation to influencing public debate, for example. It does not demean the reader by taking him or her through a step-by-step process for writing and delivering radio scripts or being interviewed by Jeremy Paxman. It would have had to be a very different – and a very large – book for people who are already exploring digitally how digital media work . . . and that area is changing so quickly that such a book would be (1) out of date before it was published and (2) not the medium ('book') such people would refer to anyway.

This book is designed to open up enquiry into how communication works. It does not explore the semiotics of advertising or the 'world-reshaping' power of art and image. It does not enquire into the effectiveness of icons – in either the ancient or the modern sense – and does not delve into the emotional complexity of music. But it raises questions about communication in non-linguistic fields and leaves the reader wanting more. That is all to the good – and is evidence of good communication, opening up thinking rather than trying to sew it all up and answer every question.

So, Richard Littledale has given us a straightforward, practical and personal book that is aimed at opening up our thinking and self-reflection on how we do what we do and how effective we think we are being when we communicate something we think matters. Furthermore, he has written a personal book. As with the particularity of any communication context or community, so communication involves particular people. And these individuals have particular histories and particular strengths and weaknesses. It is, therefore, completely appropriate that this book emanates from the particular thinking and experience of a particular practitioner: a Baptist minister, blogger, broadcaster and writer from London. He keeps his ruminations down to earth and practical – and he grounds them in and illustrates them from his own experience of communicating in a variety of media. He speaks of what he knows and does not pretend to know what he hasn't experienced. And he draws on the wisdom and experience of other thinkers and practitioners.

There is no record that St Francis ever actually said what he is (too) often reported to have said to the 'missionaries' he sent out: 'Preach the Gospel. Use words if you have to.' But this formulation does have the virtue of arresting our attention and holding together the integrity of word and deed. Words matter. Words can kill or create. No-one will not benefit from thinking through how language and communication works – and, possibly, being more respectful to how language is used in our complicated everyday lives.

Before proceeding to the journey this book takes you on, I leave you with a story. I am not an artist. I have tried to draw and paint, but have never managed to gain any confidence in either. Many years ago, I was proving resistant to even trying to draw when, on holiday with our young children, my wife (now an artist working in glass) sat me down and told me to draw the chair. I started to draw the chair. It looked like a bad drawing of a badly designed chair of indeterminate shape. The artist then asked me to try again, this time drawing the spaces around and between the solid elements of the chair. I reluctantly did so – and found that the chair emerged out of the less definite lines around the spaces. It looked more real. But it also helped me see differently by looking differently at what looked obvious.

This book will give some clear shape and helpful 'lines'. But the lasting value will come from being asked to look differently at what appears initially to be obvious and then describing differently what is newly seen. This is – to use the language with which I began – more 'godly' in the sense that it opens us up to the potential of good communication, the dangers of poor communication, and the creative, life-giving and simply more interesting exploration of the rich world of language and communication.

Rt Rev. Nick Baines
Bishop of Bradford

Introduction

As a new young pastor, I was on the train rattling my way into London. I had graduated in French and Practical Theology, and had no idea how little I knew about life. I was still feeling my way in the worlds of preaching and pastoral care, not yet appreciating how ambiguous our words can be, even when we think they are clear. As the train got closer to the terminus, we passed through the badlands of dereliction and detritus which always seem to grow up around railway tracks. There were old platelayers' huts with weeds forcing their way through the shattered windows, discarded rubbish, broken freight wagons and graffiti everywhere.

It was a piece of graffiti which caught my naïve young eyes. There on a wall next to the railway, between vandalised warehouses and soot-blackened houses, was a single word sprayed on the bricks:

Compassion?

I couldn't quite work out whether the word was an ironic contrast with its location, a plea for action or a cynical dismissal. It continued to trouble me throughout the journey and has lingered with me ever since.

Do our words articulate our environment or sit awkwardly in the midst of it, I wonder? Do they add to our understanding of the world and of each other – or are they just so much noise? The intervening years have certainly taught me the power of the right word spoken in the right context. I have seen the capacity of words to inspire, to empower and to challenge. As a pastor, it has been my privilege to pronounce people husband and wife, and to dismiss the soul on its journey at the end of life. These are auspicious words, and between us we consent to load them with meaning. I have seen the power of words to heal, to destroy, to challenge, to motivate and to reassure.

Another book of words on words?

Surely, to embark on another book about communication is to set yourself up for a fall? It is almost inevitable that it will suffer some of the very pitfalls it describes. We may live in a high-tech interconnected world, but we all know that words are still important, and we don't need a book to tell us so. The purpose of this book is not to preach – and anyway you have presumably indicated your belief in the importance of words by opening the book. Nor is the purpose to cover every aspect of the communications spectrum and to explain it all exhaustively. Such a book would be too long both to read and to write. Not only that, but by the time we had finished reading it there would be no time left to communicate anyway! No – the intention of this book is neither to preach, nor to catalogue. Instead, its purposes are threefold:

To understand

In the first instance, the aim is to understand what really goes on when we communicate with each other. What *actually* happens when a thought forms in my mind and crosses the space between you and me? What are the stages on its journey, and where do words feature in the whole exercise? If our capacity to speak is part of the image of God in us, then how is that expressed? The role of community in communication will be considered too.

To apply

A famous academic, long since retired, was once interviewed by a young reporter. She, thinking to find a new angle after all the other interviews he had given, asked him what he had done with all the silks he had been awarded at his various graduation ceremonies. With a slight nod of his head, he indicated the patchwork quilt which covered his knees. 'What matters, young woman,' he said, 'is not the learning but the application of learning.' This book, in three parts, seeks to take the theoretical understanding from Part 1 and apply it in different situations. In part 3, it then looks at what to do when communication has gone wrong. It is neither a theoretical treatise nor a simple how-to manual, but rather a fusion of the two. This list is not exhaustive, of course, but examines a number of different areas where the learning might be applied.

To improve

I'm never a big fan of those twee aphorisms which try to turn a bad thing into a good one. 'There are no strangers, only friends you haven't met yet' would be one. Another is 'there are no problems – only challenges'. In fact, there are problems in communication, and not inconsiderable ones at that. If your dearest desire is to communicate effectively, and it's just not happening, then that is a problem. This book tries to suggest some ways in which you might tackle it. By bringing in insights from the Bible, business coaching, action learning, the Church and other sources, it opens up windows to new possibilities.

If I ever meet the person who wielded the spray can on that wall beside the railway, I think I would like to congratulate them.

Who needs words?

It was wrong to vandalise the wall, of course, but that provocative word in that downbeat context was like a ray of piercing light. I've never yet wielded a spray can in anger, and probably never will. I'd like to think, though, that my typed words could provoke as much thought as those sprayed ones did all that time ago.

Part 1

The fundamentals of communication

1.1 Who needs words?

Just one step away from the manic noise and filthy rumble of overladen trucks in a busy street in Kolkata is the Missionaries of Charity orphanage, founded by Mother Teresa. Outside, all is noise, suffering and poverty, with young and old living and dying on the crowded pavements. Inside, it's a different story. Here, young lives are saved every single day. In row after row of cots, their little crumpled forms are fed, loved and protected until they find enough strength to go out through the gates and make their way in the world. Parked outside the entrance to the nursery is an enormous truck used for carrying vital food supplies. It is decked out in bright colours and has the jangly decorations and sparkly chains so typical of all the trucks on the road outside. This one, however, is different, for it carries another message. Emblazoned in huge letters above the cab are the words 'God is love'.

In that context, of course, they make perfect sense. They are as much a description of the truck's business as an advert for milk might be on the side of a dairy farmer's truck. But what do they really mean, the words themselves? Of course, they are in English, so there's no problem with the language. However, the assumption that we can understand the words does not presuppose that we understand their meaning. Every word in this simple phrase could be picked over and analysed by linguists and theologians. Ironically, it is precisely in the act of seeking their meaning that they may obliterate it. 'God' might mean any number of things, from the world-creating and sustaining deity of Judeo–Christian heritage to a wooden idol, or even a matinee idol. For some, it is simply a vague agglomeration of everything they think is 'nice'.

Moving on, the word 'is' could bear a number of meanings, from the esoteric and the obscure to the blindingly obvious. Some readers may well remember President Bill Clinton at his impeachment trial saying that his guilt might depend on what exactly the lawyers meant by the word 'is'. In our particular sentence, by the time we get to the word 'love', our heads are reeling with possibilities. Depending on our interpretation of the previous two words, we might envisage it as anything from practical concern to sexual enticement. Language is a rich, complex and often slippery thing. The words themselves, separated from the context of the Indian truck, become something of a mystery, and even the three-word phrase 'God is love' demands careful interpretation.

Perhaps we should try a simpler phrase, without any philo-sophical or theological baggage. Here it comes: 'my cat is blue'. Once again, we are faced with a bewildering array of possibilities. The writer could be referring to the psychological and emotional state of the moggy, implying that it is feeling sad. Equally, this could be a communication from one cat aficionado to another, where the word 'blue' is an instantly recognisable shorthand for 'Persian blue'. Then again, the writer could be some kind of fantasist who may also claim to own a green dog and a pink rabbit! Even the clearest and least ambiguous of words do not necessarily make everything clear and unambiguous.

Every time we communicate, from the simplest instruction to the most complex philosophical concept, we engage in a series of intricate manoeuvres across the space which separates two human beings. Let's imagine that Samantha wants to tell Fergus that the rose outside the window is yellow. Even in this simple exchange, there are numerous steps involved:

- Samantha sees the rose through the window.
- Signals from Samantha's eye travel up her optic nerve into the brain, where it registers the colour yellow.
- Signals travel from her brain to her facial muscles and her tongue, where she forms the word 'yellow'.
- Air particles in the space between Samantha and Fergus are agitated in such a way as to produce a sound wave which travels to Fergus's ear.
- From his ear, the signals travel up his nerve to the brain.
- Fergus then registers the colour yellow in his brain.

Of course, we don't know whether he is thinking of a deep, rich yellow or an acidic one. We don't even know if he is thinking of the particular flower that Samantha is describing. It is these kinds of puzzles which have made the study of linguistics and semantics so rich over the years. As soon as we start to look under the surface to see what lies beneath the words we say and the ways in which we combine them, we realise that language itself is a complex and enigmatic thing.

Sign vs symbol

Even when carefully used, language is an imprecise instrument. Essentially, a language is a code to which a certain group of people subscribe, agreeing to mean the same things by the same words. While there has been extensive debate about exactly how this functions and the sense in which a word indicates the thing it describes, most people would agree on it as a code of some description. At its simplest, this might be a set of jargon employed by the people within a certain profession. At its most complex, it is a language evolved over many millennia by a particular linguistic group, either ethnic or national. There has been extensive linguistic debate about how each word operates within any given language. Some argue that a word signifies a particular object or concept, but only in so far as it stands out from other word-ideas. Others see words as symbols, somehow depicting the properties or importance of the concept to which they have become attached. In this way, they might function rather like a computer icon – not exactly describing the thing they indicate, but giving us a clue. Thus, for instance, the Windows logo on many a computer screen may not *actually* mean that it opens a window, but, once opened, *like* a window it gives onto a view beyond it.

In general, a word functions more like a sign, pointing to the object or emotion it denotes. It is not a symbol, in that it does not sum up the object it describes. It does not function like the pictograms we see in an airport, depicting a person running from a door (for an exit), or a plane descending from the sky (for the arrivals hall). The word 'circle' does not have any of the properties of a circle; it does not even look like it when written down. Rather, it is an agreed code to denote that particular shape. Apart from onomatopoeic words, which sound like the thing they describe, words are simply a device to point to something, whether an action, an emotion, an object or a place.

Of course, once we start employing language to describe concepts rather than objects, the whole thing gets more complicated.

If Samantha were telling Fergus about how she feels, rather than about what she can see, then the communication space between them becomes a minefield which must be crossed only with extreme caution.

When a man entered a bend rather too fast in his car, he was affronted that the woman with whom he nearly collided yelled 'pig!' at him, and took it to be an insult. He was still reflecting on whether this was a comment simply on his driving or on his personality in general when he rounded the bend and slammed into the hapless hog who had parked himself in the middle of the road.

Not only do words have numerous meanings, but also the meanings attached to words change and evolve over time. If the road accident above had happened before people started talking about male chauvinism and labelling its worst offenders as pigs, it might have had a very different outcome. A happy crowd of holidaymakers might once have been described as 'gay' – but that word has acquired a new meaning that has entirely replaced the old. Equally, a young boy who, with a grin on his face, described Jesus as 'really wicked' was in fact paying him a compliment, rather than seeking an excuse to be thrown out of his Sunday School class.

Tone

A set of words, all with meanings which are broadly accepted, can still be interpreted in all sorts of ways. This is where tone comes into play. For instance, the words 'you never told me' can sound very different, depending on whether they are uttered in an accusatory or a regretful tone. Tone is combinations of volume, intonation, pitch and physical gesture which are woven into the tapestry of human communication. If you try saying the word 'welcome' out loud, once while smiling and once while not, you will find that they actually sound different. I would not have believed the difference it made until the moment when I participated in a live radio broadcast and the producer told my colleague to smile as she introduced the programme. Despite my scepticism, I could indeed 'hear the smile' in her voice as she spoke. This is not simply because the shape of the mouth is different when we smile; it also introduces a warmth and depth of tone into what we say.

Some languages, such as Mandarin, have developed a notation in the written script which indicates the tone which should be employed for significant words. As we discuss later, the use of tone is one of the particular challenges associated with radio broadcasting. Considering our tone when we communicate is every bit as important as researching our facts or choosing our words. The wrong tone can undermine the best linguistic ingredients and ruin the finished product. Even if every individual element is exactly right, the result when they are combined can seem disappointing and dull.

A friend of mine used to say that her cooking tasted lousy if it was not 'cooked with love'. The best ingredients and the right cooking times could still produce unappetising food if not combined in the right frame of mind. The same could be said of many acts of communication – the words are right and the facts are sound, but the tone is all wrong. A bit like my friend's occasionally loveless cooking, it may be insipid at best and indigestible at worst. An understanding of communication which is based purely on words is bound to be inadequate, for it tells less than half the story. We must look to how the words are said and the way that they sound to the hearer. Tone can make all the difference between winning hearers over and turning them away, and therefore repays careful investigation. As we will see in section 2.1 on preaching, a sermon, for instance, which extols all the best virtues and most wonderful properties of love can be totally undermined by a tone infused with anger.

Gesture

I used to be very involved in the theatre, especially in my school days. There was something about bringing characters and stories to life in the three-dimensional environment of the stage that I found captivating. In the story of any production, there came the magical moment when as an actor you 'knew your words', and the umbilical cord with the dog-eared pages of the script could be cut. At last the writer's two-dimensional creation in print could become a living, breathing thing on the stage. But, of course, 'knowing the words' was only half the story. A character can only live on stage, and even more in film, when words are combined with tone, gesture and movement in order to create a believable human being.

When we communicate face to face, we read almost as much from the visual information we receive as we do from the audio. In his book *Successful Workplace Communication*, Phil Baguley states that we read 10 per cent of a message from a person's words, 40 per cent from their tone, and the remaining 50 per cent from their body and facial gestures (p. 28). This is something that we have learnt from the very earliest weeks of our lives, when we first focus on the faces of those who love us. A baby staring fixedly into its mother's face as it feeds is not only expressing love but also learning a skill which it will carry throughout its life. Those moments spent reading faces, searching them for signs of love, reassurance or even fear, are a baby's first steps in communication, long before they learn about words or even about tone.

As we grow up, our focus spreads beyond just the face of the person with whom we communicate, and we begin to read the language of gesture in faces, hands and indeed the whole body. Many of the instincts we develop about certain kinds of people in certain kinds of situations are drawn from these early lessons in 'people-reading'. When people are unable to read others in this way because they are visually impaired or blind altogether, other senses deepen to fill up the void. Those who cannot see develop a sixth sense to read people through touch, or even through the texture of their voice.

These skills mean that we quickly discern if there is a mismatch between the words that are said and the gestures which accompany them. When I greet an old friend, the chances are that I will stretch out my hand to take his a split second before I utter the words 'great to see you'. However, in another context where a public figure is 'inserting' gestures specifically to reinforce a particular message, the order of word and gesture may be reversed by fractions of a second. The brains of the people in the audience pick up on this tiny mismatch and read it as insincerity. When British prime minister Gordon Brown first went on video-sharing website YouTube in April 2009 to get his message across, many felt that the oft-inserted smiles, intended to convey warmth and approachability, in fact suggested cynical manipulation. This is also the reason why some people are deeply sceptical of tele-evangelists, with their film-star smiles and their glitzy production values. They read a mismatch between words and gestures which makes them uncertain about the sincerity of the message.

When *neuro-linguistic programming* was born in the early 1970s, it drew on observed patterns of human interaction and used them to accelerate learning. It encourages communicators to read the micro-gestures employed by both speakers and listeners which form the pattern of communication in a work environment. These might range from those things usually termed body language, such as the crossed arms of the defensive or the sagging shoulders of the bored, to much smaller movements of the eyes or the facial muscles. If people looking ahead to the future tend to look up and to the right, for instance, perhaps a visionary manager could do the same in order to sell a vision to his or her team. In the context of one-to-one conversations, practitioners are encouraged to observe the gestures of the other person carefully, and to mimic them. Skilfully done, this can create an empathetic environment which facilitates good communication. We shall examine some of these principles more closely under pastoral conversations in Part 2. Others who inherited the mantle of neuro-linguistic programming have gone on to make use of it in training speakers in industry and politics to persuade not only through their vocabulary and tone, but also through their gesture, their posture and their stance.

Personality and environment

We need to be aware of the degree to which our personality affects our communications, both as speakers and as listeners. Our own life story, with its ups and its downs, has a distinct bearing on the way in which we use and receive language. The scars we bear from prior experience, together with wisdom born from it, ensure that we are constantly evolving as communicating creatures. Although language is an agreed code, two people may read a different message from the same word, as we have already seen with our reckless male driver. To this we must add that groups of people, from army units and rock bands to churches and youth groups, may evolve their own unacknowledged vocabulary born of shared experience. Eugene Peterson, whose popular language Bible translation, *The Message*, has sold around the world, says that 'You are the only one who speaks the language of your congregation, and the various "tongues" they speak – what they meant by certain phrases, what words are "loaded" from past experiences and encounters' (letter to the author).

It is because our communication is determined by our personality that communication skills are not transferable in any 'one-size-fits-all' way. Often, the disappointment people feel when a technique which works for one communicator fails to work for them is entirely misplaced. Communicating with someone else's language is like wearing somebody else's clothes – unlikely to create the right impression, and liable to be uncomfortable.

Prejudice

After all that has been said about language, it is important to state that the word 'prejudice' is being used here with no sexual, political or racial connotation. There are all manner of lesser prejudices and preconceptions which affect the outcome of the communication encounter. My feelings about a particular person will affect their ability to communicate with me, and me with them, for good or ill. The assumptions which we bring to the communication encounter set its rules and determine its efficiency. This is why a hostile setting, whether in a political chamber or a domestic kitchen, is unlikely to produce effective communication, no matter how skilful the words nor how wide the vocabulary. Often, we cannot do anything about our prejudices. They are as innate to my psychological make-up as an allergy is to my physical one. My prior experience may have conditioned me to believe that everything this person says will be either infuriating or wonderful. In fact, I may even believe those things about someone who *looks* or *sounds* like that particular person.

However, half the battle lies in acknowledging that prejudices are at work, and then reinterpreting the things we hear accordingly.

A prejudice named may be a prejudice tamed, or at least some way towards it. When training preachers, I often tell them that the most important tool in their kit is a mirror. They must understand themselves in order to understand how they hear and how they are heard.

In all of this, perhaps we should acknowledge that words alone mean very little. Rather like the words on the truck in Kolkata, they make sense only when read in conjunction with other things. The message 'God is love' on the truck clearly meant that God's love resulted in mouths being fed and lives being saved. The truck without the words would have been just another overladen lorry, but the words without the truck would have been … just words.

1.2   From Word to flesh and back again

We have already established that words form only part of the communication spectrum. They sit alongside gesture and tone, and must be read in the context of personality and environment. They can be described as signs of the objects, ideas or emotions to which they refer. Thus, for instance, the word 'square' denotes an object with four sides of equal proportions and four right angles which join them. However, we immediately encounter a problem, since even this simple word is open to numerous interpretations:

- a public space in the centre of a city or town
- a mathematical procedure whereby a number is multiplied by itself
- a philosophical procedure whereby an attempt is made to reconcile irreconcilable ideas or opinions, as in 'to square the circle'

- a pejorative term implying that a person or fashion is out of date.

With such complexity in the interpretation of a simple word, it should be no surprise that the whole process becomes even more challenging once we start dealing with complex ideas. And yet, words are the principal way in which we interpret the world. As John Berger puts it in his little book *Ways of Seeing*, 'we explain the world with words' (p. 7). This may be a vulnerable, fragile, ambiguous way to interpret the world, but it is the one we have been given.

For Christians this is especially poignant, since the Biblical narratives are clear that God spoke the world into being. In other words, the creation is seen as a product of his voice. It is this understanding which has formed the backbone of centuries of debate concerning the *imago dei*, or image of God in humankind. In what sense can we be said to be made in his image? If God is everywhere, and I can only be in one place at a time, how can I be said to be like him? If God knows everything and I know only some things, in what sense do I imitate him? If God lives forever and my life is limited by time, how can we be said to be struck from the same mould? These are complex question without easy answers. However, the description of God's act of creation through speech leads us to believe that the capacity for speech itself reflects part of God's image in us. With the exception of the creation of humankind, all other aspects of creation in Genesis chapter 1 are described as a response to the words of God, introduced with the words 'and God said …'.

Generations after the creation, with the dream of Eden but a distant memory, the Bible says that God spoke to his people again, and particularly to Moses as their leader. On this occasion, however, there was to be a written record of what he said. The remarkable thing about Moses' meeting with God on Mount Sinai was not only that he should have survived it unscathed, but that he should emerge from it with a written record of their meeting. The covenant meeting which established the people's relationship with their God was a miracle, and the stone tablets were the miraculous minutes of it. Those tablets, inscribed by God's own hand, were proof that he had not done with the people just yet. Their status as the people chosen by God to receive his written word, his special law, would keep their heads held high for generations to come, even through many persecutions.

How should we interpret it, then, when these stone tablets of holy words never made it beyond the foot of the mountain on account of the people's behaviour? Moses had no sooner arrived back at the camp than he was confronted with the unexpected spectacle of God's people worshipping golden idols which they had made from melted-down jewellery. Uncertain about when or whether Moses would return, they had made alternative arrangements. In a fit of pique, Moses threw the stone tablets to the ground, where they shattered on impact. Were the people behaving this way because they had not yet read the words, or would the words have made little difference? Would written words have left them as unmoved as spoken words appeared to do with their forebears, Adam and Eve? Whatever the answer, these shattered tablets, with their fragments of God's calligraphy scattered on the desert floor, seem to say something about the inadequacy of language in the divine encounter. God had spoken and now written to the people, but their relationship with him still appeared to be pretty shaky.

In the centuries that followed, God went on speaking – delivering his words in verbal rather than written form. Prophet after prophet spoke on his behalf, intoning God's vision for his people. Sometimes the words would be backed up by actions, like Jeremiah smashing a water pot in the public square and saying that God would likewise smash the corrupt city of Jerusalem. On other occasions, the prophets were obliged to act out their own words, like Ezekiel building a siege model of Jerusalem. Others still had to reinforce their words with their lives, like Hosea marrying an unfaithful wife to make a point about God's faithfulness. Their messages, in both word and deed, met with a mixed response. Sometimes they would provoke the odd flurry of faith, like sparks flying up from a lathe, but at other times the only result of their faithful speaking was apathy. There is something deeply symbolic about the sound of Jeremiah's voice, spoken over his shoulder as he is carried into exile, saying 'I told you so', since all his warnings about this impending fate had been ignored.

Perhaps a written word, or even a spoken one, was not enough? After many years of brutal persecution and bloodshed, the Jewish people scattered far and wide, the prophetic voice fell silent, and they were left with only their scrolls, their history and a longing for change. At last, John the Baptist broke the silence. John the Evangelist puts it simply that 'there came a man, sent from God' (John 1:6). His role was not strictly prophetic, but more of a warm-up to the main event. As a teenager once put it in a Sunday Bible class, John was the man who said 'I'm not the Messiah, but I know a man who is'. John's role was to announce a new kind of word from God. Although there was a continuum with all the things God had said before, this time it would be delivered in a new way. This time it was neither spoken nor written, but lived.

This was the incarnate word – every principle of God's love and grace enshrined within the human form of his son. The erudite John described him as the 'word made flesh' (John 1:14).

Jesus' life is a potent combination of word and deed – his words explaining his deeds and his deeds illuminating his words. In fact, the most potent authentication of his words comes in his deeds. In his death and resurrection, Jesus is in effect saying 'I told you so' about all the extraordinary promises he made. Matthew highlighted this when he wrote towards the end of his Gospel that the Christ had risen 'Just as he said he would' (Matthew 16:7).

Flesh made word

The trouble is, if Jesus was God's visible word, then those of us living in subsequent centuries have somehow missed out. If God felt that the best way to communicate was for people to see and hear this living word, then our experience is poor by comparison with those who lived in the first century in Palestine. We were not there to hear him speak. We did not stand in the crowd to watch him work a miracle or raise the dead. All our impressions about this divine word are formed on the basis of those human words which we read in the Bible. Anyone reading this book of mine has formed their impression of Jesus mostly on the basis of the written accounts of his life.

Whether we read them as inerrant Gospel truth, as historically reliable documents or as absorbing quasi-historical accounts, the Jesus whom the Christian Church presents to the world is the one with whom the Gospels have landed us. Even if we believe that his arrival was in part because of the inadequacy of words to bridge the divine–human gulf, we nonetheless have a Jesus to whom we have been introduced through ... words. Let's be clear that those words rank highly in terms of authenticity and documentary evidence. Many of them can be dated within less than a century of the events which they describe. Furthermore, the sheer volume of manuscripts gives us a high degree of confidence in their contents. There are over 13,000 manuscripts of portions on the New Testament, for instance, which is high by any standards. It is often said that the impact of the Bible on other literature is such that even if every version of the Bible were destroyed, it could be rewritten from its quotations in other literature. The words in the Bible deserve to be taken seriously. However, they are still written words. What is to say that they will not suffer the same fate as Moses' tablets of old – smashed and shattered in the light of subsequent experience?

Word made flesh again

In churches and cathedrals, youth groups and cafes, universities and schools, people are introduced to Christ, the incarnate word, as described in the written word, through the spoken word. As listeners are directed to the deeds and words of Christ, along with the prophets who preceded him and the apostles who succeeded him, this all takes place through the mediation of the language of those who are doing the telling. This happens in all sorts of ways, and not just through overt evangelism or preaching. In its own way, this was exactly what was happening in the orphanage at Kolkata, and on the busy roads outside as the 'God is love' truck plied back and forth for all to see. Very often, the story of Jesus is told through discussions and casual conversations. The incarnate word lives again through the words of his followers.

This has enormous scope for good, since the word is made flesh again in the character and life-experience of the communicator. All that we have said in section 1.1 about the interplay of word, tone, gesture and personality comes into effect here. The priceless word of a speaking God to his creation finds its voice in the myriad voices of his followers. This can be wonderful, since it means that God is heard in as many voices and is seen in as many colours and is felt in as many textures as his spokesmen and spokeswomen will allow. Their character and experience and humanity become part of the telling. However, this brings threats as well as opportunities. If I speak about the love of God with an angry tone, will his word be heard? If I speak about the precision and intricacy of God's creation in a sloppy way, will I undermine the message? That the word should be made flesh again in human words is an honour and a challenge, as we shall see.

The Word made words

Whenever writing about Christian communication, writers are torn between theology and pragmatism. On the one hand, there is a need for an exploration of the theology and theory behind communication. On the other hand, people want to know 'how to do it', so there is a need for practical explanation. This tends to lead to a 'user's manual' approach, resulting in books which tell us how to conduct a pastoral conversation, how to chair a committee meeting or even how to preach a sermon.

The intention in this book has been to bring the two together. The theology must inform the practice, and the practice questions the theology. Although Part 2 offers lots of practical advice on everything from blogging and broadcasting to pastoral conversations and worship, all must be seen in the light of our most fundamental beliefs about communication and what it is.

If we see communication as a gift from God and a reflection of his nature within us, then there is a sense in which every interchange – be it a conversation about last night's football or a discussion about the end of the world, is a sacred exchange. We are talking creatures, because God made us that way, and as such we should not take any form of communication lightly. Our stories should be wholesome, our sermons should be honest, our reporting should be accurate, our listening should be keen and our speaking should be beautiful.

Of course, this cannot mean that everything we speak *about* must be beautiful. We cannot interact with the world as it is unless we can describe its dark as well as its lighter sides. Language must serve to describe the ugly as well as the beautiful, and to address perplexity as well as clarity. Surely, what matters is how we use it? Like our creator before us, our speech should create a new and better reality than was there before we opened our mouths. This might take many forms. We might turn over a lie to expose a truth lying underneath. We might slide a wedge of hope under a door of despair, exposing a better possibility which stands on the other side. We might water the arid ground of defeat with optimism so that ideas break through like so many new shoots on a spring morning. These things apply whether your language is used in the theological seminary, in the pulpit, in the school playground or on the factory floor.

Martin Luther was a man who enjoyed using language to the full. His speech could range from vulgar jest to theological gem and back again with apparently effortless ease. There are books written of his 'table talk' – dinnertime conversations about life, the universe and everything. One of his favourite mottoes was *peccator fortiter*, or 'sin boldly' – a motto which will reappear at the very end of this book. We should never be so afraid of saying the wrong thing that we say nothing. There are undoubtedly times when silence is best, as we shall see in section 1.4. However, there is the world of difference between the silence born of choice and the silence born of fear. If our awe at the gift of language and its possibilities makes us afraid to use it, then we have rubbished the gift. Better to use it carefully than not to use it at all.

Judging by what we read in the creation narratives, if God had not spoken, there would be nothing. Full stop.

1.3   A web of words

The ability to form and receive words may be seen as a gift, a precious element of our make-up as created beings. As we have seen, it carries all sorts of possibilities, both negative and positive. It gives us the ability to create new realities and destroy old certainties simply by speaking. It equips us for creative endeavour and exposes us to careless failure. As such, this gift must be treated with both wonder and caution. Not only this, but also the gift itself is growing and changing, like a living organism. Despite attempts in some European countries to 'pin language down' and define its meanings absolutely, it cannot be done. With changing times and shifting seasons, the meaning of language moves on, and a word which meant one thing today may mean quite another tomorrow. When we look in Part 2 at different ways in which words can be combined to different effects, we are embarking on a brave endeavour filled with enormous potential. However, before we investigate the specific contexts in which words can be combined to achieve specific effects, there are some underlying principles we must understand about weaving words together.

Imagination

First, we need to dispel the notion that imagination is 'making things up'. If we see it this way, then imagination may be banished to the realm of the fairy story and the fantasy novel, and can have no part in serious exchange. However, to speak or write imaginatively is not to describe things which do not exist. Rather, it is to use language in such a way that things which always existed can be seen more plainly. As John Berger famously states: 'Imagination is not, as is sometimes thought, the ability to invent: it is the ability to disclose that which exists'.

If we are to be truly exceptional communicators, then we need to venture regularly and boldly into the realms of the imagination. Without doing so, we linger forever in the mundane, neither fully understanding what is around us nor beginning to envisage what might be. In their book *The Heart of Change*, John Kotter and Dan Cohen urge business leaders to tap into the depths of people's imaginations, since that is the place where change begins: 'People change what they do less because they are given analysis that shifts their thinking than because they are shown a truth that influences their feelings' (p. 1).

Imaginative language may be used not only to reveal the nature of those things which surround us already, but also to outline possibilities which do not yet exist. These may be anything from inventions which could revolutionise all our lives, to resolve which might break the deadlock of our personal circumstances. The ability to dream is nothing without the language to describe the dreams. Some of the most famous words in history, which still send a shiver down the spine today, do so because they touch a deep vein within our imaginative being. When Queen Elizabeth I gathered her troops at Tilbury Docks on the eve of the battle of the Spanish Armada, she told them that she was resolved 'in the midst and heat of the battle, to live and die among you all, and to lay down for my God and for my kingdom, and my people, and my honour and my blood, even in the dust'.

In speaking like that, she struck a nerve which had been struck by generals like Cicero before her and would be touched by leaders like Churchill after her. Equally, when Martin Luther King spoke to the sea of faces before the Lincoln Memorial at the Civil Rights March and told them that 'I have a dream', he struck a rich seam in the human soul which dreams beyond its physical and historical limitations.

There are many strands which account for the success of Barack Obama's presidential election campaign in 2008. Among them are his considerable learning and his personal aura. However, he also demonstrated the ability to drill deep down into the depths of the American psyche and to tap a well of imagination, creativity and hope.

Poetry

When I was at school, I was taught that there were two kinds of poetry – proper poetry, which rhymed, and blank verse, which didn't. Thankfully, my understanding of poetry is now somewhat deeper. The poet is a person who can combine words in such startling ways that the world around is seen in a new light. The poet's job is to let that light flood in on the landscape which we once thought was familiar and to reveal new contours and depths within it. The task is to open up new possibilities, rather than to pin down old certainties.

The word 'poetry' is drawn from the Greek verb *poeio* ('to make'), and the poet's unique contribution to human life is to fashion new ideas and possibilities from the ordinary things and words around about us. The poet uses meta*phor* to (literally) 'carry over' a meaning from one context and place it in a new one where both it and its surroundings can be seen in a different light. In fact, the poet is a powerful person, and metaphorical language may be just as capable of describing the world as any other form of language such as scientific or analytical. In his collection *Leaves of Grass*, published in 1855, Walt Whitman recognised the poet's unique contribution:

> After all the seas are crossed (as they seem already cross'd),
> After the great captains and engineers have accomplish'd their work,
> After the noble inventors, after the scientists, the chemist, the geologist,
> ethnologist,
> Finally shall come the poet worthy of that name.

Whitman is suggesting that the poet's contribution is at least as important as those from the scientists and others – possibly more so.

It is hardly surprising that poetic language features so highly in the work of the Old Testament prophets. Many of their words were spoken at a time of extreme angst for their audience. People had been carried off en masse from their homes, in a forerunner of the kind of 'ethnic cleansing' we know today. In strange and intimidating surroundings, they needed to look at old truths in a new light. Very little new theology was outlined during this time of exile. Rather, through skilful use of poetic language, the prophets brought the old theology to life and made it sing in the ears and burn in the hearts of their people. A good example of this is Isaiah's call to faith in Isaiah 40:21–6:

> Do you not know? Have you not heard? Has it not been told you from the beginning? Have you not understood since the earth was founded? He sits enthroned above the circle of the earth, and its people are like grasshoppers. He stretches out the heavens like a canopy, and spreads them out like a tent to live in. He brings princes to naught and reduces the rulers of this world to nothing. No sooner

are they planted, no sooner are they sown, no sooner do they take root in the ground, than he blows on them and they wither, and a whirlwind sweeps them away like chaff. 'To whom will you compare me? Or who is my equal?' says the Holy One. Lift your eyes and look to the heavens: Who created all these? He who brings out the starry host one by one, and calls them each by name. Because of his great power and mighty strength, not one of them is missing.

Isaiah is not describing any new theology in his words. Indeed, the whole point of them is that he is calling upon his listeners to remember their theology of old. Using poetic and evocative language, he is calling them back to their roots. What is new, however, is his description. His focus on the stars as evidence of God's handiwork, for instance, is a particularly appropriate way to evoke faith within the physical context of Babylon, with its predilection for astral worship.

Today, a world away from the Old Testament prophets, poetry is still to be found in the most surprising places – whether this is a giant manufacturing company talking about the 'power of dreams', or the chief executive of the world's biggest software company saying that he 'can't wait for tomorrow and I'm doing everything I can to make it happen'. The people behind these phrases have realised that the person who captures the imagination goes a long way towards capturing the soul. Furthermore, the one who catches the soul releases the best of human endeavour, creativity and energy. The workplace, which was once the bastion of hard and analytical language, has opened its doors to the softer language of poetry. This is not because it has gone soft and changed its objectives. Quite the reverse. The movers and shakers have discovered that more can be moved and shaken by carefully chosen words than they had ever realised.

Story (not fiction)

We see a similar strategy employed by those who use story as a means to engender loyalty and harness energy within the corporate world. From the international political stage to the boardroom, many have realised that a truth conveyed through story is a truth which reaches its target and changes its hearer. Executives are encouraged to 'tell their company's story' rather than simply to sell its product. Consultants are brought in to hear the story on the shop floor and reflect it back to management. Marketing experts weave a story around a product and then sell the story, knowing that the product will surely follow. As with poetry and indeed with imagination itself, creating a story does not mean that we are inventing something fictitious which does not exist. Rather, we are describing something which does (or should) exist in such a way that the human spirit is excited and energised by it. In *The Heart of Change*, Kotter and Cohen describe this as 'painting pictures of the future' (p. 67) – and they are by no means alone.

Human beings are put together in such a way that they make sense of their environment through story. This applies not only to the small stories about how a certain thing was named or how things came to be as they are. It applies also to the wider narratives, the broad backdrop against which our lives are set. This is why, in many ancient cultures, the storytellers are the guardians of collective understanding. The storytellers are the ones who pass on the collected wisdom of the past to future generations. In so doing, they stitch the past and the present together into a continuum. In numerous Native American tribes, the storyteller doll is a traditional figure – lots of little faces gathered round a mother figure as the stories are told. Humankind is a storytelling animal.

Not only this, but story increases our retention of information too. If you were to read the list of objects in the box below and try to remember all ten of them, the chances are that you would fail.

1.	Green pick-up truck
2.	Teddy bear with only one ear
3.	Tulips
4.	Red iron gate
5.	Empty pizza box
6.	White and grey pigeon
7.	Purple sandal
8.	Shakespeare's *Othello*
9.	Flute
10.	Sports bag

However, if I were to tell you this:

> In the garden behind the red iron gate, there are tulips growing all along the edge of the drive. Right in the middle of the drive is a green pick-up truck with a one-eared teddy bear sitting on the roof, a flute poking out of its little stitched mouth and a purple sandal on one of its paws. In the back of the truck is a copy of Shakespeare's *Othello*, with an empty pizza box on top of it. A white and grey pigeon has left its perch on an old sports bag and is eyeing the box hungrily

– then the chances are that you would remember far more of it.

If the stories are left behind in the infant classroom, then the best resources of human imagination and creativity will be left there too. Those who would take the gift of words and weave them to great effect need to discover the power of story again.

Parable

For many, the word 'parable' is associated with the stories of Jesus in general, and the story of the Prodigal Son in particular. In fact, parables as a means of communication were established long before Jesus came on the scene. In the Jewish world, they were allegorical stories used to describe the nature of heaven employing images drawn from earth. In the Greek world, they were moral tales, setting two courses of action side by side or (*parallel*) so that the listener could compare the two and decide upon the right one. Jesus frequently combined the two approaches, setting two courses of action side by side in order to reveal a greater truth about the kingdom of heaven.

To use parables in communicating today is to set two truths or realities side by side and to allow the listeners to draw their own conclusions about which is the better, or wiser, or more desirable of the two. This might be done in preaching, where the ethics of the kingdom and the ethics of the world are set side by side. It might be done in the classroom too, with a teacher encouraging students not just to learn a set of facts, but to juxtapose those facts with others which seem to contradict them, and see what emerges. Parables provide a means of teasing the imagination and awakening the curiosity of those who listen.

I once led a Bible study on the Old Testament book of Jonah, which tells the story of a prophet who was sent to preach God's forgiveness to a group of foreigners who were seen by Jonah and his countrymen as beneath contempt. Through the course of his adventures, he is confronted with the uncomfortable truth that no-one is beyond redemption, and that God will not withhold his love from even the most surprising people. In the Bible-study group, we had a person whose job was to teach English to asylum-seekers, who often encounter a very mixed reception from their neighbours. As he began to compare Jonah's attitude with those which he encountered every day regarding his foreign students, both leapt into sharp relief. Set alongside each other, Jonah's resentful attitude to foreigners and the hostility encountered by his students made a new kind of sense. In his one sentence 'Jonah sounds like a *tabloid*-reader', he had leapt across the centuries and made a startling parallel. This is how parables are meant to function.

Of course, this is a risky form of communication, in that the person telling the parable has no control over the outcome in the listener's mind. The parable-teller cannot tell the parable-listener what to think. That said, the scope for gain is great too. When people have grown bored of the facts or inured to the reality around them, we need to weave those facts together in a different way.

For many communicators in many settings, the thought that they have little control over the message received is a scary one. They prize clarity over creativity; and ambiguity is a dangerous enemy. However, it is also true that human beings are at their most intellectually productive when they dare to communicate across the chasm of ambiguity. When the paranoid craving for unambiguous clarity is set aside, we can dare to dream, to ponder and to sketch out new possibilities even where our ideas are not altogether thought out. Sometimes, if we rush to clarity, we miss out on all sorts of creative opportunities as we accelerate towards the goal.

The Christian Church has many centuries of experience behind it when it comes to creative ambiguity. Originally formed from Jews and gentiles, slaves and free, Romans and Greeks, it had little choice but to find a way of allowing different viewpoints to find houseroom together. Like fitting a large family into a small house, it has not been an easy undertaking. As church leaders have wrestled with everything from Trinitarian theology to sexual ethics, the wisest ones have learnt that truth is often to be found in the marshy land of ambiguity rather than on the shores of certainty. In such a place, our faith serves us well, since we trust in an invisible God rather than our immediately visible surroundings. There are lessons to be learned here about the way in which debate is conducted and truth is experienced without feeling the need for a headlong rush to unassailable certainty.

If words are a gift, the ability to weave them together in creative and exciting ways is a gift too. Like skeins of brightly coloured thread, they may be combined to create a tapestry of extraordinary and startling beauty. This was the discovery of Michel Chevreul, a dyemaker in the royal tapestry works in Paris in the eighteenth century. He discovered that skeins of pure colour juxtaposed on the tapestry would create brilliant hues in the eye of the beholder. His insights were then applied by the pointillist painting movement, where artists combined dots of pure colour on the canvas to create an overall image of sparkling intensity.

We can do the same with our words, juxtaposing them and combining them in myriad different ways to create new possibilities. This might include the creation of stories which outline the world differently, or poetry which shines a new light on an old world. Alternatively, it might involve stories or parables. All these things are an adventure in creative ambiguity, where we experiment with our words in order to create something which moves the reader or listener. Like any creative approach, there are risks involved. When Seurat and other painters first put Chevreul's theories to the test with brush and canvas, some people thought they were mad. To some, even today, their paintings are nothing more than a mass of dots. To others, who stand in awe before them in art galleries around the world, they are brilliant and scintillating works of art. Who is right? Who is to say? In the end, the world is surely enriched by those who dare to try something new, either with paintbrush or with words.

1.4   The risk of silence

Printed silence

There are many different ways we might react to white space on the printed page. We might see it as an unnecessary gimmick, a waste of space, or maybe even a welcome break from the printed word. It might serve to highlight the words which surround it, much as an artist can use the negative space around an object to depict that object in painted or drawn media. The figure below, for instance, may be seen as either a set of four black squares or a white cross. Both would be true, and the one enables us to see the other.

I visited a second-hand shop in a small town and found myself drawn, as ever, to the bookshelves. On the shelf, sandwiched between the cookery books and the DIY manuals, was a battered old paperback entitled *How to buy almost anything second-hand*. I couldn't really decide whether it was appropriate or ironic. In some ways, it feels the same writing words ... about blank space. By definition, it is impossible to use words in order to describe the absence of words, surely? However, I will say this. The space between written words, like the silence between spoken ones, allows you to appreciate the words which are spoken or written all the more. It is because of this that it will repay some time to consider silence in our investigation of communication, irony notwithstanding.

Silence between worlds

Communication gurus often talk about the importance of ensuring that the communicator's message 'lands in the world' occupied by the listener. In other words, the message received must make enough sense in that world for the listener to accept it and to invest time in processing it. Should this fail to happen, then the listener will become distracted, fidgety or even downright hostile. To ensure that this does not happen, inordinate amounts of time are spent in understanding the listener's world. This might include everything from casual conversations around the water-cooler to an exhaustive study of the company minute books. When a consultant first begins his or her relationship with a client, they may spend hours or even days in building a rapport. As well as time spent together, this might include more subtle measures, such as mirroring the client's style of speech or even their style of dress. Some of these techniques will be examined in greater detail in our investigation of pastoral conversations in section 2.3. All these things, more focused on listening than speaking, are designed to shorten the gap between one world and the other.

In her book *Preaching as Local Theology and Folk Art*, Professor Leonora Tubbs Tisdale urges preachers to undergo a similar exercise. Her background lies in social anthropology, and she urges preachers to take a leaf out of the social anthropologist's book. Like participant observers studying the social anthropology of a culture, she encourages them to study the culture of their congregation as manifested in everything from formal rituals to unwritten rules. She calls these things 'symbols of congregational life', and her list includes anecdotes within the congregation, rituals (both overt and unacknowledged), events in the church's calendar, and even the architecture of the place. All this is entirely worthwhile and can only make the communication exchange more valuable. However, there are times when passive silence carries more weight than active research. As a visitor to a foreign culture, there are times when it behoves us to shut up, put the camera down and simply absorb all that is strange around about us.

On the day I arrived for a conference in India, my journey from the airport to the hotel at 2am was an assault on all the senses – from the smells through the window to the cow staring down the taxi in the middle of the road. At that moment, the best thing for me to do was not to talk to my driver, nor to take photos – but simply to sit, listen, learn and absorb. As we explore different types of communication, encouraging excellence in speaking and writing, there must also be space for excellence in listening. Writing in France in the early seventeenth century, Bishop Francis de Sales sounded a warning that still rings true today: 'Half an hour's listening is essential, except for when you are very busy – then a full hour is needed' (quoted in Shaw, p. 17).

Your world is not the same as mine. It has different rules, a different history and a different culture running through its veins.

I cannot expect to communicate with you in that other place unless I have taken time to listen to its sounds and feel its rhythm first. Maybe this is why the writer of Ecclesiastes suggested that we should not rush to speak: 'Do not be quick with your mouth; do not be hasty in your heart to utter anything before God. God is in heaven and you are on earth, so let your words be few' (Ecclesiastes 5:2).

The silence between worlds before we attempt to cross between them is an acknowledgement of the other's right to life and independent existence. It affirms their right to be different, and acknowledges the onus on the communicator to understand the one with whom they communicate.

Silence between words

Sometimes, once that silence is over and we embark on the adventure of oral communication, we are terrified to stop. Like a person successfully riding a bike for the first time, we are afraid that if we stop, the forward momentum will be lost, the bicycle will fall over and we will never be able to pick it up and continue the journey again. Speakers must learn to be listeners, and writers must learn to be readers. This space between words, either written or spoken, oils the wheels of communication and allows the vehicle to move. Research by Strait et al. published in the *European Journal of Neuroscience* has suggested that there is a direct causal link between the ability to listen acutely and to understand emotions accurately. Basically, the article suggested that musicians make better lovers because their highly attuned sense of hearing allows them to read emotions better than other people can: 'Musical experience has been shown to enhance sensitivity to emotion in speech in both children and adults, with musicians more accurately identifying emotions expressed in speech samples'.

Of course, this doesn't mean that we should all immediately rush out and learn a musical instrument in order to find our dream partner! What it does is to provide some scientific evidence for a truth which we all know deep down anyway: good listeners make better speakers. That said, there are different qualities of listening. We have all had the experience of being listened to by a person whose eyes are darting to and fro, clearly desperate to be somewhere else and listening to someone more interesting. There is also a kind of listening whose purpose is so clearly to fulfil some agenda of the listener's that the speaker feels used. In *Conversation Matters*, Peter Shaw outlines numerous steps for effective listening, which include everything from attitude to acceptance.

These are all useful tools for the listener. However, the quality of listening which serves us best overall is the one where the listener affords the speaker that highest of human privileges – the gift of undivided attention. One of the most remarkable features of the ancient book of Job, in the Old Testament, is the relationship it displays between one man and his creator. After Job has gone through many trials and endured the ill-informed opinions of his neighbours, God steps in and demands that Job 'brace yourself like a man; I will question you and you shall answer me' (40:7). This may seem harsh or even frightening, but with those words God affords Job the highest dignity – of being listened to and taken seriously.

In all that follows in Part 2 about the different ways in which words can be combined to communicate to different effect, the value of silence should not be forgotten. Like white space in print, or the blank mount around the edge of a painting, it serves only to emphasise the bit which really matters.

The courage to be silent

Today we are constantly bombarded by messages from all quarters. Our computers spew out e-mails, our phones clog up with voice and text messages, our journeys to work are surrounded by billboards advertising every kind of product. Were we but able to see it, the air around us is in fact a thick soup of data of every kind. Upwards of a billion text messages every month are exchanged in the UK alone. In such a noisy place, silence can be an act of defiance. The call to silence, a bit like the call from the 'Go Slow' campaign to slow down our busy lives, can seem a very odd thing indeed. 'Go Slow' began in Italy – a nation famed for the frenetic pace of its language and lifestyle. What began as a campaign about slow cooking and eating spread to travel, communication and lifestyle. Since the movement began, London has held its first 'Slow Down' festival, encouraging citizens to slow down, talk less and listen more. As appealing as that might be to some, it still feels profoundly counter-cultural. Conditioned as we are to noise and bustle, the alternative can fill us with dread.

Though written many years ago, Henri Nouwen's challenge to experience our inner and often painful silence still sends a shiver down the spine of many a busy person:

> We have become so used to this state of anaesthesia that we panic when there is nothing or nobody left to distract us. When we have no project to finish, no friend to visit, no book to read, no television to watch or no record to play, and when we are left all alone by ourselves we are brought so close to the revelation of our basic human aloneness ... that we will do anything to get busy again and continue the game. (p. 28)

No noise? No distraction? How could we possibly bear it? Undoubt-edly, many of us would find it difficult – but it can be done. Not only that, but it should be done. The person who would communicate through words should maybe learn to endure the silence first. Having done so, the words will be more thoughtful and more precious.

The creation narratives which tell us that God created the world also tell us that there was silence before the world began. In other words, the created order with all its mountainous beauty and its microscopic intricacy arose out of ... silence. The most creative words ever spoken were preceded by a silence of indeterminate length. In fact, we are unable to measure its length, since neither time nor clocks were invented before the sound of the creative voice. If such creative things can arise from the silence, then we should not be afraid of it, surely, when we try to communicate?

1.5   Speaking the unspeakable

We have considered the capacity for human speech as a gift to the human race. We have considered the ways in which words, gesture, silence and tone can be combined to outline the world in great detail and scintillating contrast. The gift of language, however, would be poorly used if it were employed only to describe those things which we already see. Historically, it has been not only the poet but also the prophet who acts as wordsmith, hammering out a new and shining future on the anvil of the present. This does not mean that a prophet is involved purely in the business of prediction, describing things before they happen like some act in a travelling show. A prophet's role is to shine a piercing light on the now as well as the then. Indeed, sometimes it is the very brightness of the light shone on the events and people of now which casts long shadows into the future.

In Biblical terms, the most profound prophetic insight was born out of the deepest suffering. Many of the finest prophetic insights emerged from the bitter experience of exile. Popularly dated between 598 and 538 BCE, this involved the Jewish people being transported en masse away from their homes and into Babylonia. In such a situation, with the people torn up from their roots and forced to live in a far-off land where the language was unfamiliar and the customs terrifying, the prophets were the only ones who could make sense of it all. They took the theology of the past, held it up to the light of experience in the present, and shone the refracted beam onto the future.

It was their words, often combined in strange and surprising ways, which kept the people's hope alive through generations of deprivation and hardship. Jeremiah gave the people hope, even as they were carried away into exile, that the day would come when the nightmare would be over. In fact, it fell to him to describe God's new covenant with his people, which would be 'written on their hearts' (Jeremiah 31:22). Much further on into the exile, with the Jews billeted in refugee camps along the Kebar River, it was Ezekiel who painted a vision of a fiery, spectacular God who would one day return to their midst. In a day of clouds and despair, his description of God as 'like the appearance of the rainbow in the clouds on a rainy day' (Ezekiel 1:28) must have encouraged many.

Twenty-first-century prophets?

Some theologians draw parallels between the Jews' experience of exile and the experience of Christians in the twenty-first-century Western world. They point out that Christians, like their Jewish forebears, find themselves adrift in unfamiliar territory where their customs and even their language seem out of place. Like the Jews of old, they need to cling onto the beliefs of the past and articulate them in the present so that their faith will survive into the future. Walter Brueggemann, in particular, is an advocate of this approach. He traces the echoes of the prophetic voice down through the centuries, calling them 'cadences of hope', and believes that they find a ready home in the twenty-first century. He believes that the experience of Christians in a post-Christian Western world is their own kind of exile: 'By exile I mean to practice faith in a cultural environment that is at least indifferent to those faith claims and perhaps hostile' (interview with *Mainstream* magazine, Summer 2001).

The parallels are certainly striking, and there are lessons to be learnt from those who have gone before, in terms of articulating their faith in a hostile environment. However, if we exploit the parallels either too far or too lightly, it can prove to be a damaging experience both for those who speak with a prophetic voice and for those who are obliged to listen to it.

A fortress mentality which sets Christians against the wicked world 'out there' leads to a kind of communication which breeds fear and misunderstanding. Those who fear they will be misunderstood often end up fulfilling their own prophecy, because their message comes out in a garbled mixture of jargon and arrogance which alienates their listener straight away. If I am convinced that you will reject what I am going to say anyway, then it can make me very careless in the way I communicate it. Equally, if I think that you are so spiritually dull or so antagonistic to my beliefs that you are bound not to understand them, then I will make little effort to help you understand them when I speak. If I have convinced myself that you are fundamentally opposed to the beliefs which I hold dear, then the communication space between us becomes so infused with hostility and fear that any reasonable communication becomes impossible. It is true that many Western European nations have moved away from their former Christian heritage. This certainly requires great care in crossing the communication gap. However, if Christians simply shout louder to guarantee a hearing, people on the other side will just turn away and go in search of more peaceful conversation elsewhere.

In such a context, those who call themselves prophets may actually court controversy and relish opposition as proof of their spiritual authenticity. Accusations of bigotry, arrogance and intransigence bounce off them like pebbles thrown at the armour plating of a tank. Like the tank, they advance remorselessly, crushing everything before them and leaving many things flattened in their wake. This does not mean that there is no place for the prophetic voice. What is needed is the ability to express prophetic insight in such a way that others will feel inclined to listen to it.

Confident humility

I once found myself called to account for my faith before a panel of students on a 'Religion in modern Britain' course at my local teacher-training college. Sitting alongside me were a rabbi, a Buddhist monk and a Muslim hospital chaplain. We were all asked the same series of questions, each answering for 'their' faith in turn. When it came to the question on 'the greatest dangers facing your faith today', I found that two words leapt immediately to mind: arrogance and timidity. The Church in the United Kingdom stands in danger of an arrogance born of precedence – 'we were here first'. However, it faces an equally grave danger of timidity. Afraid to be seen as dogmatic, it would rather keep its faith to itself, even in a time of spiritual hunger. It is often people of other faiths, especially Islam, who are shocked at the reticence of British Christians to talk about their faith.

All too often, this fear of saying the wrong thing, or even of saying the right thing in the wrong way, leads to a kind of awkward silence. Instead of a creative exchange, there is a nervous silence. People with faith are afraid of speaking in case they sound arrogant. People without it are afraid of listening in case they get sucked into something they would rather avoid. The space which should be full of creative banter is instead left unoccupied, a sort of uneasy no-man's-land where no-one but the extremists dare to tread.

There must be another way, surely, to talk about these precious things? People who would speak of their faith need to do so with a kind of confident humility. Because they are confident of their beliefs, they are happy to share them, and even to expose them to scrutiny, without fearing that they will be destroyed. With all humility, these convictions are offered up to the international and intercultural conversation of faith and philosophy without feeling that this places them in any danger. The people who can do this are confident in their beliefs, but humble enough to know and accept that not everyone will agree with them. They are both confidently humble and humbly confident.

If people are afraid of such an exchange, then their faith may be a very brittle thing. Dogma has taught them that they must feel equally certain of every tenet of their faith, with no exceptions. This means that if any one of those beliefs crumples under scrutiny, then the whole edifice comes tumbling down and the soul is left exposed, like a snail without its shell. A faith which is so fragile is of limited value, surely? Better to be humbly confident of what you believe, and to accept that others will not necessarily feel the same way. If faith is let loose in the marketplace of ideas, we have to believe that it can look after itself and not be drowned out by the competition. If a belief is fundamentally true, its truth will out without our help or protection. Though he was hardly renowned as a great champion of reasoned and even discourse, Charles Spurgeon's description of the Bible as a lion which simply needs to be let out of its cage, without anyone needing to fight for it, may help us here. If what we believe is true, then it is true because it is true, and not because we believe it. We need neither fear for its safety nor insist on its special status and privilege. The Apostle Paul, who never seemed lacking in conviction or certainty, nonetheless wrote the words that love does not 'insist on its own way' (1 Corinthians 13:5).

A vision described

All around us, there are people equipped with extraordinary vision. Some can see life-saving inventions not yet built. Others can see sources of renewable energy on which the future of the planet depends. Still others can see solutions to the deepest heartache of those they love. The trouble is, no-one will benefit from those ideas unless they can communicate them. It's all very well seeing the invisible, but we have to depict it, to communicate it, if anybody other than the one with the vision is to benefit. This is where we need communities of communication. We need places where our half-caught vision can be described without derision. We need places where our half-baked ideas can be given time to rise, and then to bake. Communication without community is impossible.

1.6   Truth through community

The Christian Church is a community of communication, where its fundamental message is spoken, shared and experienced. Not only this, but it has lessons to teach both about the creative possibilities of ambiguity and about the importance of *experiencing* truth. Time and time again in the New Testament, the litmus test of faith is not academic argument or doctrinal statement but ethical behaviour. In other words, the right question to ask about Christian conviction is not just 'is it clear?' or 'is it plain?' but rather 'does it work?' In his epistle, James is particularly forthright on this, asking the straightforward question as to what good it is if 'a man claims to have faith but has no deeds' (James 2:14). A faith which could only be expressed in words was, quite simply, inadequate.

However, it is not just enacted faith in the life of the individual which is seen as a test of authenticity. There is a powerful communal element too. The shared life of the Church is seen as a proving ground for the reality or otherwise of its convictions. Thus, in Philippians 1:27, Paul can urge the young church in Philippi to 'live a life worthy of the Gospel of Christ', choosing as the word for 'live' a specific verb (*polittheusneo*, from which we derive 'politics') which refers exclusively to communal living. Equally, the church in Corinth, with its squabbling and jealousies, put in jeopardy not only its own work but also the continuing witness of the Christian Church throughout the ancient world. Then, as now, bad news travelled fast.

The emerging church in the first century had great barriers to overcome. Within its ranks, it had slaves and slave-owners, Romans and Greeks. In the church at Philippi, to which Paul addressed his advice on the importance of communal life, there were people from all echelons of Roman society. There were sailors, merchants, wealthy slave-owners and former slaves. To worship and serve together meant breaking all kinds of social taboos and rewriting the rule book on how to live together.

In many churches, Jews and former pagans needed to worship together. The contrast between these groups was especially acute. For the strictest Jews, even the most casual contact with a gentile was a corrupting influence. The fear of the other was bolstered by myth and rumour. Thus, many Jews were taught that gentile girls menstruated from birth, thereby rendering them ritually unclean from the start. This was nonsense, of course, but it helped to keep up the dividing wall between the two groups. Against such a backdrop, the challenge to the Church to communicate its message so well that people not only lived different individual lives, but different communal lives too, was immense. The ancient world was watching to see whether this really was truth through community or whether it would prove to be falsehood by division.

Although the cultural landscape has changed out of all recognition, the challenge is still there. Churches now include people from every faith background and none. They may include those who have lost their jobs, and those who fired them. In any church, bankers, teachers, refuse-collectors and the unemployed may worship alongside each other. Occasionally, people on two sides of an industrial dispute will find themselves standing alongside each other, singing the same hymns and drinking from the same chalice. There were churches in parts of the United Kingdom during former miners' strikes where that was exactly the case. These churches must be loci, surely, for determining whether truth through community is actually possible?

In any discussion of communication, it is important to note that the test of authenticity is about not only data transferred but also actions inspired or behaviour changed. Margaret Thatcher's former head of press relations apparently used to tell his staff that if 'they didn't hear it, you didn't say it'. Their protestations about how clear their press briefings had been were of no interest to him so long as the wrong message was being printed in the papers the following day. In a Church context, we might be tempted to say that if 'they don't do it, you didn't say it'. In the end, communication is not just about the words spoken but also about the words heard and what people do with them.

This means that those reviewing communication both in churches and elsewhere need to look to their 'communication culture'. This culture may comprise many elements, including the obvious ones such as vocabulary used, as well as less obvious elements. The communication culture may be shaped by the clothes people wear, the rooms in which they work, the way in which they pass messages to and fro, and even the way they park their cars! All these things may serve to oil the wheels of communication, or alternatively to make them fall off.

Thus, a school which promotes an ethos of positive affirmation and engendering the best in its students needs to promote just such a culture in its staffroom too. Backbiting and point-scoring in the staffroom will affect morale and performance in the classroom. Even an accumulation of one person's unwashed coffee cups in the sink may cause such aggravation that the real business of the school is impaired. It's not enough to say that the students and parents will never see inside the staffroom and therefore it doesn't matter. If communication is about more than words, then a negative atmosphere in the staffroom will leach out into the classroom and beyond, just as surely as a bad smell can find its way through walls and floorboards.

And what about those working in the communications business? Sometimes their technology and equipment may be state-of-the-art but their communication culture renders it worthless. Some years ago, I was trying to obtain a piece of research commissioned by a giant telecommunications company on the subject of ... communication. It took three phone-calls to three separate departments before eventually being passed on to the warehouse, who said that they thought they might have run out of copies but they weren't sure. In that moment, the value of both the research and the technology instantly dropped by several notches. If the research on how to hold conversations could not be found, or delivered, then it had little purpose. Conversely, the computer communications giants who have re-engineered their work spaces to allow for social interaction and fun have found that it has a notable gain in terms of creative output. Happy and communicative staff tend to be creative staff, which means that they are also productive.

We could look to the broadcast industry too. Within it, there are thousands of hard-working people committed to delivering the highest standards of broadcast media to a global audience. Many hours may be devoted in the edit suite or the recording studio to producing material of which they can be proud. That said, it only takes a small piece of office politics, a bruised ego or a trampled personality to ruin everything. The broadcast industry is no more prone to this than any other. However, when their finished product is communication, it means that internal communication difficulties expose them to particular criticism.

Then there is the dark underbelly of the fashion and beauty industry. These clothes and products are all about making us look as beautiful as we can possibly be. They are designed to show us off to our best advantage and make us attractive to the world.

Thousands of pounds and hundreds of working hours are devoted to creating objects of beauty. Sadly, the catfighting *off* the catwalk, and the scandals surrounding size-zero models, have contrived to spoil much of that work. A beautiful outfit which is the product of so much ugliness can seem like so many shabby rags. When the fashions trickle down from the catwalk to the high street, they are often only made affordable by the abuse of underpaid workers in sweatshops on the other side of the world. No amount of advertising can expunge the guilt we feel at wearing a garment which is the product of human misery. Every part of the operation, from the design studio to the catwalk to the factory floor to the high street, contributes to the communication culture.

Communication in industry, which once centred around plant and equipment, now seems focused on relationship and community. Companies are as likely to bring in an expert to reprogramme their relationships as they are their computers. Communication is about more than words or even actions; it is about connection. This understanding has given rise to the growth of the 'coaching' business, with its focus on personal strengths and releasing potential. Managers are encouraged not only to ensure that their communiqués to staff are clear, but also that they understand the staff to whom they are sent. A message which is crystal clear to the person who sent it may be confusing, or even threatening, to the person who receives it. The perceived threat may have nothing to do with the words themselves, but everything to do with the manner, the tone, or even the room in which they were delivered. We are back to the communication culture again.

Set against the backdrop of contemporary business coaching, the words of a twentieth-century Russian Orthodox priest might seem a strange place to end Part 1 of this book. However, in his little *Diary of a Russian Priest,* perhaps Alexander Elchaninov could see into the future when he wrote: 'Every sermon pronounced only with our lips is dead and false, and those who listen always unmistakably feel it'.

Despite all that we have said about the careful selection of words and the way that they are invested with meaning, the words alone are not the whole story. Even if we believe language to be ennobled by its divine origin, this does not guarantee its success. We must choose our words carefully, by all means, but our success or failure will be determined by many factors beyond our vocabulary.

Part 2 of this book will take us from the pulpit to the studio, from the intimacy of the counselling room to the untold millions on the Worldwide Web. We shall think about communication as a means to comfort, challenge, stimulate and inspire. In all of this, we shall look at communication as a whole, where words play an important but not an exclusive role.

Part 2

The practice of communication

2.1 Preaching

Somebody once described an after-dinner speaker who 'laboured under the illusion that if he went on long enough he might become interesting, rather like an ugly person who thinks that if they stand around long enough they might become beautiful'. Sadly, of course, both would be deluded. Many preachers are lured into thinking that just because they have a captive audience they also have a captivated one. In many cases, nothing could be further from the truth. People come to church hungry for an electrifying encounter with God, and leave after a stultifying encounter with the preacher. To address all the contributory factors in this state of affairs would take a series of books. However, here are some worthwhile pointers to consider. ·

Multiple listening

God

As noted in Part 1, good speaking is always preceded by good listening. However, the preacher must develop the art of listening in several directions at once. First and foremost, she or he must learn to listen to God. Without a prayerful life and the ability to hear God's voice, the preacher has nothing more edifying to pass on than their own opinions and prejudices. There must be discipline within the preacher's life to create time and space where the voice of the divine can be heard. Useful techniques include a regular daily time of prayer and a structured reading of the Bible entirely unconnected to the preparation of sermons. Medieval monastic tradition observed four stages in the process of reading Scripture:

1. *lectio*   the reading aloud of the Bible
2. *meditatio*   visualising the passage through the use of all the senses
3. *oratio*   concentrating on God in prayer
4. *contemplatio* awaiting God's revelation.

This is not about preparing sermons; this is about preparing the preacher. It is about turning that man or woman into a creature who soaks up the mind of God just as easily as a plant soaks up the sun. This does not happen overnight; and good habits of listening to God can take years to perfect.

Church

A preacher who wishes to connect with his or her congregation must take serious steps to understand that congregation, or else that preacher's words will fall on deaf ears. At its simplest level, this might consist of knowing what kinds of songs the congregation like to sing in church and what newspapers they read. However, there are all kinds of underlying habits, half-remembered myths and unwritten rules which lurk beneath the surface of every church. As mentioned in section 1.4 above, these are the features of church life outlined by Leonora Tubbs Tisdale in her book *Preaching as Local Theology and Folk Art*. With her social-anthropological training, she highlights the need to look for such things in order to read the church, just as one might read a foreign culture. Every one of these things tells a story about what kind of church it is and repays careful study for the would-be preacher. On arrival in a new church, this means that the preacher needs every sense finely attuned to such signals all around. What do the posters on the wall, the half-finished conversations and the significant exchange of looks tell about this particular group of people? Of course, the listening process goes on long after the initial arrival in the church. As time goes by, moments chatting over a cup of tea or around the hospital bed can all be invested to render the time in the pulpit more useful.

Self

To say that preachers need to spend time listening to themselves does not necessarily mean that their iPods should be packed with their own sermons (although listening to your own sermons can undoubtedly be a worthwhile exercise). What is envisaged here is more the need to develop a good understanding of yourself. The preacher might be a contemplative person – brought closer to God through prayer and meditation on their own. They might be an active person – brought closer to God by serving him in active ways. Alternatively, they might be a relational person, brought closer to God by relationships and conversations with others. Understanding all these things will certainly affect the way that you preach. There also needs to be an awareness of your left-brain or right-brain bias. A left-brain bias leans towards the scientific and analytical, whereas a right-brain one inclines towards the creative and imaginative. Either can equip the preacher admirably, but it is important to know which one you are, and to preach accordingly. All too often, a jolly raconteur in daily life becomes a dry academic in the pulpit, or a serious scholar tries to behave like an entertainer in the pulpit – both with equally disastrous consequences. The preacher who strives to listen to God and to the congregation needs to listen to himself or herself as well.

Deep reading

Like a translator poring over a source document in order to really understand it before the translation begins, the preacher needs to invest serious time and energy in the business of understanding the Bible. This means reading it with a critical eye, and maybe even passing it through a series of filters such as:

- *The genre filter*: what kind of material is this? Is it Old or New Testament? Is it poetry or prose?
- *The cultural filter*: to what extent is this text the product of specific elements of its original culture? Is that culture in evidence, either above or below the surface of the text?
- *The tonal filter*: what is the tone of this piece? Is it encouraging or discouraging? Is it challenging or comforting?
- *The semantic filter*: what kind of language is being used here? Is the vocabulary chosen for special reasons? Is this a long connected argument of carefully constructed sentences, or a pastiche of small phrases like verbal graffiti?

Once the initial reading has taken place, and careful notes have been made, the preacher then needs to turn to reference works. These should be neither exclusively old nor exclusively new, and should be taken from a variety of theological flavours so as to provide balance. Not only that, but they should be read with discernment, so that the preacher neither swallows them uncritically nor dismisses them casually. Only after this careful reading will the preacher have something to say which can be said to be truly *informed*.

Humble speaking

Some may be surprised to see the word 'humble' in this section. Aren't preachers, after all, in showbusiness? Don't they relish the opportunity to be out there in front of a hungry congregation, with people hanging on their every word? In some ways they do – but then again, a preacher who is driven purely by the desire to have others listen is a lethal weapon. The effect can be to unravel churches and twist spirits into the preacher's own form without the slightest flinch. Humility is the shield which protects the congregation from the preacher's ego and the preacher from the congregation's adulation.

A preacher needs to maintain a sober and appropriate perspective on their own importance in the whole business of God speaking to people. This is only one way in which God does it, and theirs is simply the privilege to be one link in a much longer chain. In order to maintain this perspective, the preacher needs to pray for divine guidance before and during every sermon. That preacher needs also to remember that the spark of holy wisdom he or she saw in the Bible during their time of preparation will only turn into a flame when the Holy Spirit blows on it. Without the Holy Spirit, the preacher is just a speaker, and his or her message is … just a message.

Careful speaking

Of course, a preacher who is too careful may be a liability in other ways. A sermon laced with so much caution and underpinned with such a fear of offending that it doesn't really say anything is no use to anyone. The care, in this particular instance, should be applied to the tone rather than to the contents. As outlined in Part 1, human communication extends beyond the purely verbal. This means that we will read the face and gestures of the preacher as well as their words. It also means that the preacher's tone can underline or undermine what is being said. A bored or uninterested tone can make the most carefully crafted sermon in the world seem dull and uninteresting. Equally, an aggressive tone can make even the most positive of messages unpalatable. This angry tone is a particular pitfall for preachers, since the passion they feel for their subject can often transform their voice unwittingly. As the passion rises, the throat muscles constrict, the preacher is forced to exert more lung power to get the words out, and soon the sermon comes across as an angry barrage.

I once attended a conference for preachers, and the first plenary session consisted of a sermon by a well-known preacher, after which the assembled body were invited to comment. The sermon was on the story of Mary's act of love in washing Jesus' feet and drying them with her hair. It is a tender moment in the Gospel story, and shows a real act of love on her part. The preacher's sermon was well crafted and written, but there was a fundamental flaw. When the time came for questions and comments, I tentatively raised my hand and said 'the sermon was on love, but your voice was so angry that I couldn't hear the message'. He was very gracious about it, and accepted the comment with good humour, but it has stood as a warning to me ever since.

Translating?

In many ways, the role of the preacher is analogous to that of a translator. Like the translator, a preacher seeks to understand the source text of the Bible and the cultural background from which it has emerged. Like the translator, the preacher will invest hours of time and maybe lots of money in understanding every little detail of the Bible's culture so as to know what it meant *then*. Like the translator, the preacher will then invest similar amounts of effort in understanding the *now* of the congregation, so that the message can be carried from one to the other without losing too much impact on the way.

Here's the problem, though. A good, commercial, dynamic translation can slip unnoticed into its target language, and like a chameleon it can take its place in its new environment without arousing too much suspicion or shock. Surely, though, this cannot be said of the Bible? If the preacher succeeds so well in translating the Bible that it sounds harmless and unthreatening to its contemporary audience, has this not gone too far?

Eugene Peterson, whose dynamic Bible translation *The Message* has now achieved global success, nonetheless has a sober view of its achievements. 'I did not make *the Bible* easy to understand,' he told me, 'I made *the language* easy to understand.' In one sense, the sermon should always 'land' in the listener's world as an alien visitor – full of provocative questions and bearing a message from afar.

Expectancy

One of the things which sets preaching apart from certain other kinds of communication is its expectancy. Preaching does not expect simply to convey information or impart knowledge – it expects to change people. A preacher who simply leaves an impression with the congregation of a job well done has failed. The story is told that, at a reception after the first performance of Handel's *Messiah*, a woman complimented him on his masterpiece, saying that she 'enjoyed' it. Handel was not best pleased, and replied: 'Madam, I didn't write it for you to enjoy, I wrote it to make you different'. The same could be said of preaching – and it is for this reason that great preachers will repay careful study for any communicator. Like some of the great political orators, the preacher's sights are set very high, trying to be clear and endeavouring to be interesting but above all expecting to make a difference. For this reason, the preacher's motivation is high, and expectations soar. Those looking to study passionate and motivated communication for any field will find the pulpit a good place to start.

2.2   Worship

In his 1957 radio play *All That Fall*, Samuel Beckett tells the story of a Mrs Rooney on her journey to and from the railway station to meet her husband. Along the way, she bumps into numerous characters including a neighbour, Mrs Fitt, who does not recognise her. Mrs Rooney expresses her amazement, since the two of them had knelt and prayed together at the altar just the previous Sunday. 'Oh but Mrs Rooney', replies Mrs Fitt, 'in church I am alone with my maker, are not you?'

In that small exchange lies one of the complexities of worship as an act of communication. Is a worshipping congregation simply a collection of individuals going about their private worship in the same space, or is it something else entirely? Should we be more concerned in an act of worship about the invisible God who is the object of our adoration, or the visible worshippers themselves? It is a perennial problem for all those involved in the conduct of worship to recognise that it has both vertical and horizontal dimensions.

The questions regarding worship do not have simple answers, and it is certainly not the aim here to produce a comprehensive guide to the nature of worship as communication. Furthermore, the Church's concept of worship has evolved so differently down the different branches of its family tree over the millennia that it would be hopeless even to try listing all the different approaches. Instead, I shall mention some key aspects of communicative worship, which can then find expression in different ways along the low- to high-church spectrum.

Anchor

Corporate worship must be anchored in the life of the community in which it takes place. While historical heritage is an important aspect of our worship, there must nonetheless be some kind of link with the place where people actually live, the language they actually speak and the issues which actually concern them. If we do not do this, then the church becomes an island adrift in the cultural ocean, rather than part of the cultural mainland. This really came home to me when I visited a church in north-eastern India. It had been founded by British missionaries almost 100 years before, and within its doors nothing had changed. Outside the church was a swirling melee of life, noise and, above all, colour. Inside the church, almost everybody was wearing grey or black, the voices were hushed, and the hymns were as dour as the expressions on the faces of those singing them. Worship certainly doesn't need to ape the culture in which it is based, but nor should it ignore it.

There are numerous ways in which worship may be anchored in its cultural environment. In traditions where the worship is conducted in the vernacular, this is one obvious way. Even where it is not, there are ways to acknowledge the culture beyond the church in the conduct of worship. These may include artistic depictions of the world beyond the doors, and indeed the actual architecture of the church. Windows in a church, for instance, serve not only to let the light in but also to let the church see *out*. It may also affect the clothes worn by worshippers and clergy alike. Do they reflect the church's context, or set it apart? And what of the intercessory prayers of the church? They may express a real connection with the church's context. On the other hand, they may be so anodyne as to be universally applicable in any church in any historical or cultural context. While it is important that a church's public prayer should reflect the language and preoccupations of its history, there should also be room for its present. A church which only prays about needs in far-off places, but never about those around its own doorstep, for instance, is surely missing something.

Aspiration

Of course, worship which simply reflects the world around about us has significantly failed in its aim. Surely, worship is intended to draw us towards what *might be*, and not just declare what *is*? When the Jews in the desert saw the rich red, gold, blue and crimson woven into the tabernacle, they caught a glimpse of the hidden majesty of God. When a desperately poor worshipper in communist Russia saw the doors in the iconostasis open and the priest come through in his spectacular garments, that worshipper was reminded that there was more to life than the prosaic reality which the state had created. In an attempt to communicate a relationship with its earthly environment, worship must not lose touch with its heavenly goal.

One of the ways in which we achieve this is through the church's music – although there are few things more likely to cause discord within an otherwise stable congregation than to mess with its music. I used to preach in a small church where a new hymn book had been introduced with modernised words for the old hymns. Unfortunately, there were some who disapproved – and would make their disapproval plain by singing the old version of the words at the same time as everybody else sang the new ones! This is not how music and song in the church is meant to function. Instead, it should be used to unlock the depths of the soul and tap the farthest reaches of the imagination. We need songs which describe the greatest, most sublime blessings which heaven can offer, and we need music which makes us feel like singing about them. This may be done either in the spiky and provocative lyrics of more socially aware modern worship songs, or in the sublime beauty of a choral evensong. Whichever it may be, the church's music should express a longing for *something better*.

There is a place, too, for poetry without the music. As described in Part 1, the word 'poet' comes from the Greek verb for 'to make', and suggests that the poet's job is to describe the world in such a way that new possibilities are made out of old realities. Often, there is a suspicion in Christian worship of any poetry whose source is either outside the Bible or outside the church. Why should this be so? Paul himself saw fit to quote a pagan poet in order to make his point – in Athens, citing in all probability Epimenides of Crete: 'in him we live and move and have our being; we are his offspring' (Acts 17:28). Should this not make us feel that there is a place for poetry in the church's worship? And, if there is a place for poetry, then it might be that the God-ward longings of the secular poet are as apt as the assured theology of the Christian poet. After all, as God pointed out to Moses, it is God himself who gave us the ability to see, hear, describe and imagine (Exodus 4:11). Hearing spiritual longing expressed from a perspective outside the church can actually enhance the faith of those within it. When the church becomes some kind of ghetto, hermetically sealed from the world, familiarity with the things of God can breed contempt.

The place of the visual arts in Christian churches varies enormously – from the highly decorated grandeur of a Gothic cathedral to the spartan purity of a Quaker meeting house. To some, the stained-glass windows are silent teachers, inspiring their worship in ways that words cannot do, while to others they are distractions which verge on the idolatrous. There was a time when many of the world's greatest artists were to be found within the church. However, like teenage children whose rock music and fashion no longer suit their parents' tastes, they sometimes find that they are not welcome back to church with their fancy ideas. A gulf of suspicion has opened up between church and the visual arts, and it will take trust and risk on both sides to bridge it. If it can be done, then worship might be enhanced by the reintroduction of the visual into what can now be a very verbal environment.

As emphasised in section 1.4, we should not underrate the value of silence in the communication spectrum. When worship seeks to express our highest aspirations, and to focus heart and mind on an infinite and powerful God, silence may be the most eloquent communication of all. To move from speaking or singing to silence in worship may be not an admission of defeat but an act of highest adoration. There is a touching depiction of quiet worship when we read in Luke's Gospel that the Virgin Mary 'treasured up' all these things in her heart (Luke 2:19). Literally, the original Greek words mean 'collected together' and are used to describe what happens when waters from several places all flow into one place and build up. Sometimes, a quiet moment to puzzle over the mysteries of God's actions can be the most powerful kind of worship of all.

Common

To say that worship should be common is not an indicator of the kind of language we should use. Nor is it a suggestion that we should necessarily use the *Book of Common Prayer*. Something common is something which is shared by many people. A common was the place where all the people (or 'commoners') were permitted to graze their animals. A common language is one which unites many people, and a common cup is one that is shared around. We certainly do not want to encourage the kind of situation described by Mrs Fitt and Mrs Rooney above, where the common act of worship united them so little that one was not even aware of the other.

The role of music is vital in ensuring that worship is a truly common experience. It should be one of those elements of worship which brings people together, regardless of age, Christian experience or rank. Sadly, though, that is often not the case. Music which is designed for soloists or professional musicians, for example, is ill-suited to congregational singing. Music with rapid key changes, or songs with lyrics which barely fit the tune, are exclusive rather than inclusive. People who try to sing them but fail will not try a second time. While it is important to refresh the musical worship diet of any church, so that the experience of worship does not grow stale, there is nonetheless a novelty threshold for any given occasion. Too many unfamiliar songs, for instance, on one occasion, will simply put people off.

It will put them off, too, if they cannot hear what is being said or sung. Preachers and pastors who refuse the offer of a microphone where a sound system is available often do it out of a false sense of pride. 'I don't need it', they say – when all along it was not for their benefit they were being asked to use it. Inadequate amplification is a surefire way to ensure that worship is not a truly shared experience. How can people participate if they do not know what is going on? I was once leading a carol service, but had a problem with my hearing at the time. I did not dare sing out those wonderful tunes, lest my dodgy hearing meant that I would be horribly out of tune. If we can draw people into worship through something as simple as maximising the acoustics where we do it, then it should be done.

Of course, if you can hear what is going on but cannot see the visual aid which everyone is talking about, then this may be just as exclusive. I'm a big fan of visual aids, and use them wherever possible. I believe they allow me to engage both right-brain and left-brain people with the worship and preaching. This does not apply, of course, to the visually impaired. I have preached an introduction to the Book of Revelation using three great paintings. It simplified a complex book, gave people a helpful introduction, and lodged in their memories because of what they had seen. At least, it did for most of them. One woman in the congregation, who could hardly see the screen let alone what was on it, did not find it so helpful.

Even where there is no such impairment, it is important to ensure that the layout of the church does not impede visual participation. A pillar between the worshipper and the speaker will doubtless inhibit that worshipper's sense of inclusion. Equally, a shaft of bright sunlight which regularly falls across the screen where images and words are projected will help no-one. These very practical issues have to be addressed in order to give vent to our creative ambitions. It is no good wanting to move with the times by tacking on new techniques and bits of equipment if the fundamental layout of the church inhibits it. Expanding our creative repertoire in worship can only help the church. However, we must ensure that in so doing we are not undermining the nature of common worship.

Creativity

The worship of God has always attracted some of the most extraordinary creative gifts of the human race. Architects have designed great soaring cathedrals, stonemasons have built them, goldsmiths and silversmiths and embroiderers have ornamented them and composers have filled them with music. Where such cathedrals have taken several generations to build, people have lived and died while adding to this ongoing act of worship.

Sometimes, the creativity which we pour into it may not even be seen and heard by others – but that is not the point. It may be tucked away in the thoughtful selection of songs to sing or the careful crafting of words to speak. It may even have been expressed by the laying of audio cables carefully out of sight to ensure that everyone can hear. Hidden creativity is still creativity. For centuries, no-one knew about the amazing diversity of fauna which lived at the bottom of the ocean in all its bizarre beauty. It was still there – part of God's creative legacy to Planet Earth, even though nobody could see it. Johann Sebastian Bach built into the manuscript of some of his finest works the shape of the cross in a musical 'signature' at the start of them. No-one would hear it, and only the most eagle-eyed musicians would notice it – but it was there all the same. It was a small gesture of hidden and exquisite creativity. Worship should attract our creative extravagance in the best sense.

2.3   Pastoral conversation

The clue is, as they say, in the name. These are called pastoral conversations because they reflect the pastoral, or shepherding, intentions of the person conducting them. The word itself has come to have a particular association with the Christian Church, which still retains the imagery of the shepherd every time a bishop carries his 'crook'. Jesus described himself as the 'good shepherd', and in so doing was picking up on a well-established image of shepherds as the leaders of the people. In fact, he specifically described himself as the 'good shepherd', in contrast to the bad shepherds of the past who had shown scant regard for the welfare of the 'sheep' in their care. Centuries before Christ, the prophet Ezekiel had described the leaders of Israel as poor shepherds who had not 'strengthened the weak or healed those who are ill or bound up the injured. You have not brought back the strays or searched for the lost' (Ezekiel 34:4).

Anyone who has ever spent any time around sheep will know that they are stubborn and wilful but also very nervous. It doesn't take much to 'spook' a flock of sheep – whether it be a change in the direction of the wind, a stray dog on the loose or a stranger crossing their field. Since the aim of pastoral (or 'shepherdly') care is to benefit these vulnerable creatures, then the aim of pastoral conversation must be likewise. Since it is intended to benefit the 'sheep', then everything from the environment and the vocabulary to the tone of voice used must contribute to that aim.

Environment

Of course, it is not always possible to choose the environment for a pastoral conversation. It may end up happening at the school gates as the children are pouring into school, or in the stockroom at work when a stock-check suddenly turns into a heart-to-heart. However, where possible, you should always choose to conduct a pastoral conversation in an environment where the concentration is on the two people involved and nothing else. Conducting it in a public space, where people passing by can speculate as to the conversation's content, will not be helpful. Equally, a room dominated by the trappings of work may well turn a pastoral conversation into a discussion of working practices, which is not what was needed.

Chairs should be set close enough together to provide good eye contact and facilitate quiet conversation without invading the personal space of the other. In general, a V formation, or a variation of it, will provide the best environment, since it allows the two people to see each other clearly without enforcing an uncomfortable degree of direct eye contact. Teas or coffees can be a help, not least because it gives nervous hands something to do in holding a cup or mug. Never omit the box of tissues either – the moments it takes you to go off and find some elsewhere could be all the time it takes to lose the magic of the conversation.

Mirroring

Many Christians are deeply sceptical about the idea of mirroring in pastoral conversation, not least because the phrase finds its origins in psychotherapy in general and neuro-linguistic programming in particular. Basically, mirroring involves the subtle imitation of your interlocutor in everything from tone and syntax to gesture and even to dress. Thus, if the person to whom you are speaking tends to speak in short, staccato sentences, you do the same. If their sentences are long-winded, illustrated at great length with stories and anecdotes, then you take your cue from them and reply in kind. If, while they are speaking, they fold their arms across their chest or cross their legs at the ankles, then you do the same. This takes the 'body language' of old one step further, and urges us not just to observe what the other person is up to, but also to imitate it. The aim is quite simple. By mirroring the other person in this way, we are sending subtle signals to their brain that we are not quite as strange or as threatening as they might otherwise have perceived us to be. In this way, a bridge of trust is rapidly built between both parties, and the conversation is far more likely to have positive outcomes for both of us.

Of course, there are objections to this. Done clumsily, it can be painfully obvious and can make the other person feel that, far from wanting to put them at their ease, our intention is in fact to mock them. Some may also object on the grounds of dishonesty – isn't this some form of cheating by another name? Aren't we simply pretending to be like the other person in order to achieve the desired outcome? This is, they claim, just a cynical form of manipulation. Perhaps that depends on its intent. When Jesus spoke to the religious experts in discourse peppered with allusions to the prophets, but to the common people in stories full of farmers and publicans, was he being manipulative ... or just clever? The Apostle Paul was clearly an exceptionally able communicator, speaking with ease to Jews and Romans, to crowds and small gatherings. That said, he was something of a chameleon, his communication style practically changing with every stop on his tour of the ancient world. In Psidian Antioch, for example, with a largely Jewish audience, he laced his preaching liberally with quotes from the Old Testament. In Athens, on the other hand, he began his address with an allusion to their pagan statuary, and included a reference to a pagan poet. With both groups of people, the intentions in 'mirroring', or conversational adjustment, were entirely honourable. Remember – pastoral conversations are all about the sheep.

Meta-mirror

Another technique gleaned from neuro-linguistic programming is the meta-mirror. Using this technique, the 'client' is encouraged to examine their situation from a number of different points of view in order to achieve the maximum understanding of it. Let us suppose that Samantha is having difficulties in her marriage to Gordon, and has gone to speak to her friend Anita about it. After an initial chat, Anita encourages Samantha to get up so that they can move the chairs around a bit. Using this simple 'geography' in the room, Anita can encourage her friend to look at things differently.

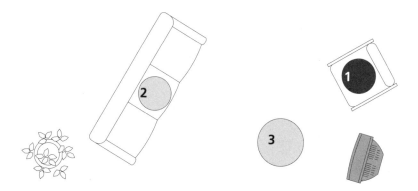

In the figure above, the furniture is placed as it might be for an all-too-typical argument between Samantha and Gordon at the end of a long day. Samantha is perched nervously on the edge of her chair (1), while Gordon is stretched out on the sofa (2) trying to watch the television. In the first stage of the meta-mirror, Samantha needs to sit in her 'usual' chair and articulate how she feels during one of their rows. All the feelings of anger, frustration and fear can come out here – indeed, it is healthy that they do so. In this and every stage, Samantha is encouraged to speak out her feelings directly as she feels them, rather than articulating or clarifying them. Thus, for example, at this stage, she would be encouraged to say 'I want him to listen to me, but he looks angry before I start', rather than 'maybe he doesn't want to listen, and I should let him watch the TV'.

In the next stage of the meta-mirror, Samantha is encouraged to cross over the room and occupy 'Gordon's' sofa. What does he see as he looks across the room at the armchair? Does he see an anxious woman afraid of him, or does he simply look past the armchair trying to see the television beside it? Using the technique described above, where she expresses the feelings directly rather than 'processing' them first, she may find herself saying surprising things such as 'can't you just leave it for a bit?' or 'why does she have to look so afraid of me?' Of course, Samantha cannot actually get inside his head; but the change of physical perspective can help to bring about a shift in mental and emotional perspective too.

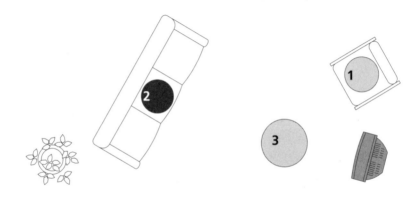

However, the exercise is not over. In the third stage of the meta-mirror, Samantha is encouraged to take over Anita's position where she has been standing apart looking at both Gordon's sofa and Samantha's armchair (3). This is an entirely new perspective. She has heard Samantha speak for herself from the armchair, and she has heard Gordon speak for himself from the sofa. What do they sound like? It may be that they are in fact expressing two sides of the same coin, since they both feel similar things. What would Samantha say to these two now, if she had them sitting there before her? Very often, this stage will bring forth huge insight and a heartfelt desire to put things right.

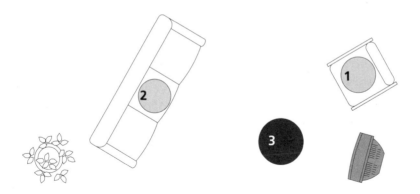

There are two more stages to go. Next, Samantha must stand a few paces further back still (4) and look at herself in Anita's former position (3). What insights has that 'version' of Samantha gained which the 'old' Samantha in the armchair, or even on the sofa, could not see? How does she feel about the situation now? Is she better able to cope, or feeling more balanced about the whole thing? She may now feel more balanced or stronger because she is in possession of new insights which she had never had in her 'habitual' armchair. The exercise is completed by Samantha quickly returning to the armchair where she started, still retaining the insights she has gained from the other positions, and looking across at Gordon's sofa differently as a result.

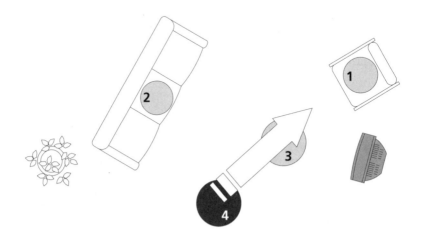

To perform this in depth takes years of training and expertise. Some may feel uncomfortable with such an 'artificial' exercise. However, the insights can help all of us in attempting to bring the best to the pastoral conversation. They teach us the value of imagination, for a start. They also show the value of a physical displacement to facilitate a mental and emotional shift. At the very least, they encourage us to place ourselves in the position of the other, and to understand things from their point of view.

A fellow pastor used to have a little message opposite his desk on the wall which would face him when he was on the phone to a person who was angry or distressed, or which he might see when that person came to visit him. The card bore just three letters, and read 'OFM'. It stood for 'one fact more', and reminded him that if he knew just one more fact about the person to whom he was talking, he might understand their angry or irrational behaviour. Even without all the elaborate techniques of the meta-mirror, it was a reminder to put himself in their position.

Vocabulary

Very often, a pastoral conversation, whether at work, at school, at home or in the church, takes place when at least one of the participants feels acutely vulnerable. They may feel attacked, ashamed or simply 'brittle'. On account of this, the person who takes the initiative in the conversation needs to pay careful attention to their vocabulary. A question phrased in the wrong way may sound like an accusation. A suggestion may be perceived as an instruction and be either rejected out of hand or followed without question by a person in a highly suggestible state. This does not mean that we should tread on eggshells so much that we end up saying almost nothing in case we say *something* in the wrong way.

However, it does mean that we select our vocabulary carefully. Questions should be phrased in as open a manner as possible. Thus, we might ask Samantha whether she has thought about broaching things with Gordon, rather than saying outright 'have you told him …?' Equally, the suggestion that she might find a time to talk to him other than when he first gets home might be phrased as 'some people find it works best if …'. Of course, this won't work for everybody, and some would always prefer very straight talking, even in the most delicate of circumstances. The rule of thumb here is that it is the person in need, rather than the other participant, who dictates the tenor of the vocabulary used.

Touch

As mentioned in Part 1, the spectrum of human communication goes way beyond words. It extends to gestures, facial expressions, tone and body posture. When we are in a vulnerable state, one of our most critical senses is touch. The wrong kind of touch can make us recoil and clam up. The right kind of touch can bring more reassurance than hundreds of words. In pastoral conversations with a person we know, most of us have a sixth sense about when it is right to back up our words with a hug or a hand on the shoulder. We should not trust that sixth sense blindly, though. Rather, in a highly sexualised society, we need to recognise that physical touch may be fraught with danger and ambiguity. When we are talking to someone we don't know, or when the situation is a more professional one in the workplace, it can be especially difficult. In such a situation, we must do as much as we can to 'read' the person before we cross over from words to physical contact. Even when we do so, we must be sure that the touching employed does not in any way abuse the person's heightened vulnerability owing to their emotional state. Touch must never be for the sake of the person 'in charge' of the conversation, nor must it be of a sexual nature. If the kind of touch we are employing could be interpreted by anyone stumbling upon the conversation as untoward, then it should not be employed. The rule of thumb here is probably 'if in doubt, don't'.

Aim

Many of the insights of psychotherapy, or the techniques of neuro-linguistic programming, can help us to think more carefully about the nature of pastoral conversations. They can lead us to pay attention to everything from gesture and vocabulary to tone and geography. However, for Christians, there is another dimension to all of this. Christians do not believe that the greatest help they can offer is drawn from their own resources. Rather, they are constantly seeking to point the other person in the direction of eternal resources which cannot be exhausted. In the words of Dietrich Bonhoeffer, they are pointing people away from the *penultimate* (our experience of now, with all its frustrations) and towards the *ultimate* (our hopes of eternal life yet to come, with no limitations). Furthermore, true pastoral care seeks not only to comfort people where they are, but also to move them on to a better place. That better place may be one in which their destructive habits are stilled or their inconsolable grief is consoled. Christian pastoral conversations have an agenda, even if that agenda is simply to hear what God is saying or to see what he is offering.

2.4 Learning and teaching

I once visited a major Victorian reconstruction in an industrial town in north-west England. There were reconstructed shops, penny arcades, vintage posters, and penny-farthing bicycles leant up casually against the shop windows. The top attraction, though, for which you had to both book and pay, was the 'Victorian School Room Experience'. We all filed in, adults and children alike, and took our places at the rickety, undersized desks. The schoolmaster, resplendent in mortar board and gown, marched to and fro across the front of the classroom, barking out angry commands and occasionally bringing down his cane on the desks for no apparent reason. Titters in the back row, not least from the grown-ups present, were dealt with sharply, and one or two had to stand up behind their undersized desks with hands on heads, bringing the desks crashing to the floor as they did so. On the latter, I speak from personal experience. It was funny because it was meant to be, and we could safely laugh at it because we knew education is no longer done that way. Or, at least, it's not done that way in schools. In businesses, churches and seminaries it may well be – and, if so, we are the poorer because of it.

Must I?

Winston Churchill, who was nobody's fool, but reputedly something of a pest at school, is credited with the phrase 'I hate to be taught, but I love to learn'. Given his broad interests in ancient and modern history, military strategy, art and other topics, he presumably learnt how to learn without the intervention of teachers. Particularly with adult learners, there can be an overwhelming pride which stands in the way of learning in any formal environment. We don't like to look stupid in front of our peers, we don't want to wallow in our own ignorance, and we definitely do not want to go back to school. This can be seen in other contexts too, such as a dance class where some are more willing to participate than others, or a church Alpha course where participants are wary of exposing their spiritual ignorance to others. In an age of Biblical illiteracy and widespread ignorance about Christian heritage, this is an issue which the church needs to tackle. If people need to learn, but do not wish to be taught, how will we bridge the gap?

Learning on the job

The 'belong–believe–behave' model, pictured opposite, accepts that people will come into the church from all kinds of backgrounds, and operating under all kinds of moralities. On first contact, the church can neither expect them to believe what the church believes nor expect them to behave as the church behaves.

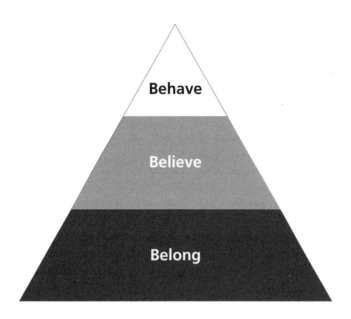

However, as the sense of belonging deepens, so does the curiosity about what the church believes and the inclination to behave as the church behaves in terms of Christian morality.

It is at the second of these phases that the greatest of learning opportunities exist. Very often, it is while people serve alongside each other, whether mending the church guttering or pouring the church coffees, that the most natural opportunities for learning occur. Here are the triggers to talk about what the church is and isn't, how we perceive our fellow human beings, and what Jesus understands about service and humility. Very often, the real teaching about what it means to be a follower of Christ takes place far from the sight of a pulpit or lectern. A practical task can lead to discussions about God's provision or the relative importance of a physical building. A testing session with a youth group can provide fruitful discussions on how we perceive the image of God in difficult settings. A practical visit to a person in need can throw a whole new light on Christ's words about 'feeding my sheep'.

This, surely, is exactly the kind of teaching and learning employed by Jesus. In much of his work, he followed the traditions of the rabbis who had gone before him. Theirs was not an education based upon classroom one-way learning. Instead, rabbi and students travelled from place to place together, learning from their different encounters along the way. To travel with a great rabbi was regarded as a high privilege, and the prayer that you might be 'covered in the dust from your rabbi's feet' was an indication that learning was, quite literally, 'on the hoof'. If Jesus had asked his disciples to undergo a theological-college training programme before they joined him 'on the road', he would have been crucified before their mission together could begin. Instead, they travelled around – sometimes together and sometimes apart. On occasions, he would entrust them with responsibilities almost beyond them, and then patiently answer their questions about how things had gone. At other times, he would teach in public and then give them a private 'teach-in' afterwards to ensure that they had fully understood the message. Even when they reported their failures to him, such as demons they had failed to drive out, he took the chance to explain things to them. This was teaching which did not seem in the least school-like; but their learning was manifest. When they were identified some time later as those who had 'been with Jesus' (Acts 4:13), the success of Jesus' approach was clear.

The importance of interaction

Interaction, clearly, is the name of the game. This applies when people are serving alongside each other, but also in the more overt learning setting of a discussion or study group. In such a setting, the leader has a delicate tightrope to tread between a degree of research and expertise which gives people confidence, and an openness which makes any and every question permissible. The need to avoid being dismissive cannot be over-emphasised here.

I heard about a man serving as a missionary in a very tough overseas setting. When asked by his pastor what had led to him doing such a thing, his answer was simple: 'It all started because, when we first began to talk about Christianity, you did *not* laugh at me when I asked whether Jesus was a spaceman'. Taking his question seriously, no matter how outlandish it might have seemed, made all the difference. As we saw in Part 1 above, a climate of intolerant certainty can really squash a spirit of open enquiry and the learning which flows from it. The more that those of mature faith can mingle with those of little or none, the better it is for everybody.

More about skills than knowledge

Mark Twain is credited with saying that 'Education is what's left over when you forget all the things the teachers made you memorise in school'. If that is true, then what do we remember from our education? We may remember our friendships, the underlying principles which were absorbed when we weren't looking, and the teachers whom we particularly liked or trusted. The lessons we remember most from any context are those which are reinforced by relationship and shared experience. This is where the communities of communication, described in Part 1 above, become so important. It is also where the kind of feedback settings described in Part 3 will come into their own. We can only learn, about communication or anything else, in a place where we feel safe to make mistakes and where yesterday's mistakes can be recycled into tomorrow's triumphs.

The teacher's tools

Wherever teaching and learning take place, there are clearly certain things to bear in mind.

Tone

A teacher's tone must indicate a degree of expertise which makes the teacher worth listening to, but must never betray a superiority which discourages the learner. The tone set, whether in the classroom or on the job, must never be dismissive, but rather should encourage question, analysis or debate.

Balance

A teacher needs to strike a balance between leading from the front and coaxing from behind. Sometimes the teacher is more of a lecturer, standing out front and delivering information and insight of which the students are currently ignorant. Other times, the teacher is more like a sports coach, watching and coaxing from the sidelines while the students put their own expertise to the test.

Action

The most effective learning is almost always associated with action – whether that action is practical, verbal or scientific. Effective action requires careful listening to see what is needed, and thoughtful action then leads to further listening.

The cycle depicted opposite may be applied to almost any kind of learning, in almost any kind of setting. As the learning

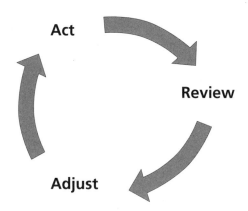

progresses through the cycle, and understanding grows, so different questions are asked at the review stage. This leads to new adjustments, which in turn leads to better actions, and ushers in a whole new set of questions.

In truth, this is not so much a circle as an upward spiral.

Outcomes

In almost every educational setting now, it is customary to establish 'desirable learning outcomes'. I remember great amusement when these were first introduced to a watercolour painting class, attended primarily by elderly ladies and myself. Teacher and students seemed nonplussed by what was expected, and in the end we settled for 'improving our painting'. However, at least it made us think. Were we there simply for the company, did we expect to turn into J. M. W. Turner overnight, or was our expectation somewhere in between? Every act of teaching, no matter what its setting or content, should have an outcome in mind, even if that outcome is simply to 'learn more'. It keeps the teaching focused, and helps to ensure that both teacher and student gain from the experience. This applies even to the kind of 'on-the-job' teaching described above. If I hope that my session of mending the church guttering will actually teach something about the value of practical service to my co-worker, then I should have that in mind even as I ascend the ladder.

Attitude

In the end, the greatest tool in the teacher's toolkit is an appropriate attitude to those whom they teach. This attitude is a mixture of excitement at the potential in their hands, and respect for the humanity of their student. It is an attitude which preachers, as well as teachers, need to cultivate. William Maltby, the then President of Methodist Conference, gave the following advice to aspiring preachers: 'Do not look down on your congregation – they are not there' (cited in *The Preacher*, no. 130, July 2008, p. 30).

The same might be applied to teaching in many contexts. Looking down on those you teach is unlikely to enhance either teaching or learning.

2.5 Mission

Mission?

Having grown up in the 1970s, I cannot read the word 'mission' without hearing the theme tune of *Mission Impossible* playing in my head, followed by Peter Graves stating that 'this tape will self-destruct in five seconds'. That, of course, is one of many interpretations of the word. It may refer to a space exploration project, a corporate strategy document, a military strike or the sweeping ambition of a huge multinational company to put a PC with their software on every desk in the world. A mission, surely, is a strategy or project to take something into a place where it has not previously existed? This might be a particular brand of soap, a political doctrine or a religious faith.

It is in this last area that most thought has been given to the need to communicate the message in such a way that it neither loses its authenticity nor alienates its audience. In his book *Contextualization in the New Testament: Patterns for Theology and Mission*, Dean Flemming puts it like this: 'In contrast to either a homogenizing globalization on the one hand or an atomizing relativism on the other, Scripture models a dynamic interaction between the local and the global which has important implications for our time' (p. 311).

If we adopt the *homogenising globalisation* approach, then every church and expression of Christianity looks the same, regardless of its context or origin. We may step into a church in anywhere from Ouagadougou to Oregon and find a liturgy and hymnody which is the same regardless of how alien it might be to the world outside the doors of the church. If, on the other hand, we adopt an *atomising relativism* approach, then a Christian from Oregon visiting his Christian cousins in Ouagadougou may find what goes on around him so entirely tied to a particular cultural expression that he barely recognises it as Christian. This cultural particularity may be expressed in everything from the clothes people wear to the elements of their worship.

Exilic faith

As the tree from which Christianity grew, Judaism had prior experience of expressing itself within an alien and unforgiving environment. In the sixth century BCE, Jewish people were forcibly expatriated to Babylonia in a move later referred to as the Exile. This was a strange context indeed for these monotheistic believers. Their overlords were Zoroastrians and star-worshippers. Instead of the familiar walls of Jerusalem around them, there were the great soaring palaces of Babylon. Coming from a background of monotheistic image-free faith, it must have been quite a shock to see the pantheon of winged creatures, evil eyes and the like which were depicted in their new home. The great prophets of the Exile, men such as Isaiah, Jeremiah and Malachi, continued to encourage an authentic faith in one everlasting God. However, their language showed clear influences from the context in which they now lived, with Isaiah describing a God 'enthroned above the circle of the earth' (Isaiah 40:22). This reflected a kind of cosmology typical of the Babylonians. Malachi talks about the 'sun of righteousness rising with healing in its wings' (Malachi 4:2) – apparently a reference to the winged disc often depicted on Babylonian buildings brooding over scenes of terrible destruction. Neither prophet was equating God with these world-views, but rather describing him within them. These are expressions of a historic and recognisable faith but in a culturally particular language.

The ministry of Jesus

Jesus was a Jew, born to a poor family, in the occupied territory of Judea in an era of local political ferment in the Roman Empire. Although he frequently quotes the Jewish scriptures of old, something we see especially in Matthew's Gospel, his stories are drawn from his immediate context. They are populated by the kinds of people who lived in this uneasy land of occupation: publicans, corrupt tax-collectors, tenant farmers, tradesmen and moneylenders. The great Jewish teachings of old had not been expressed in these terms before. Although the prophets occasionally resorted to stories, they tended to dwell more in the poetic and the esoteric. In a context where the trappings of faith were barely holding up as a bastion against the onslaught of Rome, Jesus chose to dwell on the little details of faith-inspired life. This, surely, is contextualised mission par excellence.

Paul

Paul, likewise, was raised a Jew. Early in his life he would have been selected for rabbinical training, at which he excelled. He continued in similar vein, learning the Scriptures inside out, receiving the finest religious education and rising to the heights of the Jewish establishment. Once recruited for the Christian cause, we might have expected him to adhere to a traditional form of Jewish teaching, delivered only in synagogues and substantiated only by allusions to the Old Testament Scriptures. While it is true that in Jewish towns and cities his teaching always began in the synagogue, that is where he ceases to perform to type. He preached and taught in every kind of place, from Greek debating chambers to Roman prisons. He adopted every kind of approach too. In Psidian Antioch, for example, we see him quoting extensively from Old Testament Scriptures. In Athens, on the other hand, we see him quoting from a pagan poet and using a pagan statue in order to prove his point. While his essential message remained the same, his approach varied enormously. As he put it to his friends in the church at Corinth, 'I have become all things to all people, so that by all possible means I might gain some' (1 Corinthians 9:22). Here we see a targeted and contextualised approach to mission from one of its greatest captains.

The *Heliand*

When people talk about the complexities of expressing a distinctive Christian message in a culturally mixed environment, we can be lulled into thinking that this is a modern challenge. However, as we have seen above, it has been around for a very long time. Some time in the ninth century, an anonymous German writer made a contextualised translation of the Gospel known as the *Heliand*, now sometimes referred to as the Saxon Gospel. This is an authentic retelling of the story of Jesus, but in a distinctively Saxon context. God is described as 'our Chieftain', for instance, and his dwelling place as 'the meadows of heaven'. On the night of Jesus' birth, it is 'horse-servants' who are summoned to see him, rather than shepherds, since shepherds were not in prominence at the time. Furthermore, when the wise men fall down with joy in the stable, they are described not as kings or magi but as 'thanes whose hearts became merry within them'. To us this may seem strange or even quaint, but it represented a serious attempt to dress an authentic Gospel in distinctively Saxon clothes, so that it might be all the better received. If mission is about taking something into a place where it has not been seen or experienced before, then this Saxon trailblazer may well have some lessons to teach us.

Not just words

So far, the focus has been almost exclusively on words. However, as we have seen in Part 1, the human communication spectrum is far broader than words alone. This means that when we talk about 'mission' we must be prepared to check everything from vocabulary at one end to dress and eating habits at the other. The Christian missionary community is still divided over this issue, with some maintaining all their distinctive features from their sending culture, and others adopting the dress and habits of the country to which they are sent. At one end of this scale was the great missionary Hudson Taylor, adopting the pigtail hairstyle and peasant clothing of his neighbours in China, much to the shock of his missionary colleagues elsewhere. At the other were the missionaries I met who were building a plush 250-seater state-of-the-art church in a Slovak village where some houses had neither phones nor mains gas. Wherever particular agencies sit on this issue, they acknowledge that there is gain and loss at either end of the spectrum, as depicted below.

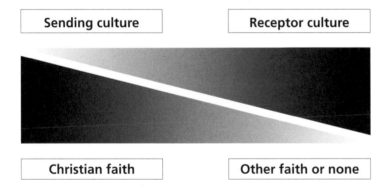

Wherever our sense of mission may take us, either across continents to share the Gospel or across corridors to pitch to another team, we would do well to be aware of some of this. A sensitivity to the culture into which we are going can save all kinds of heartache and smooth the path for our particular message. That said, there will be gain and loss, whichever 'side' we come down on when contextualising our message, whether it leads us to blend in or to stand out.

Mission insights

Whether our sense of mission comes with a small or a big 'm', there are insights for us here.

Listening as investment

People with big mission ambitions in any field are often men and women of action. They like to make good decisions, outline a clear plan of action and then get on with the job, often while leaving the competition behind. However, it is important to take a leaf out of the church's book and underline the value of listening before acting, and even before planning. Such time is not wasted but invested. With typical pithy wisdom, Jesus expressed all this with stories about a man planning to build a tower and a king preparing to fight a battle – both do well to invest in forward planning. You can find the stories in Luke 14:28–30.

Core, not trimmings

Since some adaptation will be needed along the way, it is vital to clarify at the outset what is the immutable core of your belief and values, and what might be negotiated or adapted in the interests of contextualisation. These are not easy questions, and the church will undoubtedly be divided over them until its particular mission is over. However, a sober analysis of what is core and what is peripheral to your ethos may give a different perspective on your particular mission.

Persistence

If the Christian Church struggles with identifying its core and its peripherals, it nonetheless has an enviable record in terms of persistence. The church's mission is definitely a long-term project. To date, the Christian Church has invested centuries of blood, sweat, tears and toil in its mission. William Carey, an early Baptist missionary to India, invested ten years before he saw anyone embrace the Christian faith. This man, Krishna Pal, later penned these words in his hymn, 'O thou my soul':

> Ah! No – when all things else expire,
> And perish in the general fire,
> This Name all others shall survive,
> And through eternity shall live.

Long-term goals indeed. Those who are disappointed when their particular mission does not yield short-term gain could learn much from men like William Carey and Krishna Pal.

Stage goals are still goals

To say that Carey's mission only yielded fruit after ten years would be a gross misrepresentation. In the intervening years, he healed many people, befriended others and rescued many from different kinds of oppression within their society. Even without Krishna Pal's conversion, his mission was still producing worthwhile results. This has often been the case where Christian mission agencies have built hospitals and schools, without ever seeing anyone embrace the faith which led to their construction. People are still being healed and educated, and those are worthwhile fruits in themselves. It is important to celebrate the value of stage goals on their way to the ultimate goal. So, for instance, if your end goal is to sell 10,000 items to your client, but on the way you have to build a relationship of mutual trust and respect with him, that relationship may have some value in and of itself long before the goods are shifted.

To return to Peter Graves for a minute, the *Mission Impossible* team always seemed to accomplish their mission, usually by the skin of their teeth, and often armed with every kind of disguise and gadget imaginable. Back in the real world, few of us have such an arsenal of tricks at our disposal. However, to emulate their success rate in terms of accomplishing our mission would certainly be something to aim for.

2.6   Written media

For written media u need just about zilch – in fact a computer with a (halfway decent) spellchecker is all you knead!

I hope the 'sentence' above is enough to convince most people that there is more to writing than meets the eye. It may be English, but it is neither elegant nor comprehensible. That said, there is something unnerving about writing on how to write. It feels rather like writing on how to paint, in that it might just produce the very result it seeks to avoid. Pick up any book on painting – and, after the chapters on equipment and technique, it will use the rest of the pages to tell you about the importance of developing your own technique and style. After all, many of the artists whom we admire the most are those who broke with the tradition of their time and did it their own way. When Monet first started splashing vibrant, moody colours across his canvases, the artistic establishment was so offended that the Academie Française refused to display his work. Picasso's iconic work, too, broke with just about every tradition. Crowds may flock to see his *Guernica* now, for instance, but at the time few understood what he was getting at. True greatness in art is often to be found when the rules are made up as the painter goes along. It is often the same with writing.

Writing is at its most engaging, fluid and informative when it reflects the author's own particular style. While this is not an excuse to write poorly researched material or to ride cavalier over the conventions of writing, it reflects the realities of the book-buying marketplace. Popular novelists develop an enormous following – fans will buy each book the moment it hits the shelves without having any idea of its contents. The reason for their purchase is quite simply that they like the author's style. If pushed, they may even struggle to say why. It may be a combination of vocabulary, sentence structure, tone and overall feel. Even where authors break with convention, they still develop a following. Any advice which follows below relates to principles alone, rather than to style.

Questions

Though I am disinclined to use Rudyard Kipling's description of questions as 'six honest serving men', it is undoubtedly true that they are the author's best friend. Asking the right questions before putting pen to paper or fingers to keyboard can save a lot of heartache and revision later on. These questions may seem obvious – but asking them is a vital step, whether you are writing the parish newsletter or the next bestseller.

Who is it for?

Is it for people who are familiar with your topic, or who are being introduced to it for the first time? Is it for people whose range of language and vocabulary is broad, or narrow? This is why newspapers have style guides for their writers – precisely because they have done their homework in terms of knowing their audience. They know what else (if anything) their readers read, what kinds of films they watch and what their televisual viewing habits are, and they probably have a good idea of their family income too. If you've ever wondered why companies are so willing to give you something for nothing if you'll just fill in a questionnaire, this sort of postcode-based information is invaluable to anyone who is trying to gain your attention or gain access to your wallet.

Even if you think you know who you are writing for, it may only be at the 'top level'. If you say, for instance, that you are writing for Christians – what sort of Christians do you mean? Are they new to the faith, or dyed in the wool? Are they well schooled in Christian terminology, or is this all an entirely new language to them? The answers to these questions will be still further altered by denominational affiliation and style of church. Age profile has an effect, too, since words evolve in their meanings over time. A computer-literate generation, for example, may read about the spread of a 'virus' in a very different way to their pre-computer forebears. Having asked some of these questions, the book which you were writing 'for Christians' may now be 'for Christians between the ages of 30 and 50 who have been worshipping in Anglican churches for less than two years'.

The 'who' question may also need to address the primary language of your readers. Even if you are writing it in English for an English-speaking audience, is English their first language? This is something I had to bear in mind when contributing to a Bible handbook. Although the book was written in English, it was intended for a worldwide audience, and therefore the language had to be made as straightforward as possible. To write in plain and accessible English does not mean 'dumbing down' your text, but it may involve critical authorial decisions. The onus is on you as author to be clear, rather than on the reader to be clever.

What is it for?

Is it written to entertain, to inform, to challenge or to persuade? The sharper the answers are to this question, the more focused your writing will be. When I came to write a Masters' dissertation on preaching, I thought it would be fine to write something about 'preaching in the twenty-first century'. How wrong I was. If I had stuck with that topic, I would still be researching it by the time said century was over. Instead, I had to define a particular aspect of preaching, and then find a specific question I could ask about that aspect. Only in this way could the topic be refined in such a way as to make it both manageable to write and interesting to read. While this kind of advance planning is standard practice in academic writing, it is of considerable benefit in all sorts of other writing too. A tightly focused writing project, which has excluded subject material as well as included it, will maximise its impact.

Even when writing for a recognised genre, there may be different purposes within it. Thus, for example, a newsletter might appear to be for information, but then again it might also be intended to persuade. An example of this would be a local political information sheet – which purports to be about local events and amenities, but is actually intended to generate support in forthcoming elections. You might think the purpose of a novel was purely to entertain – but what if it is intended to challenge a particular perception or tradition? There are plenty of novels where that is the case.

Even with this book, there have been questions to ask. Was its aim to inform about best practice, to outline fundamental principles, or to encourage innovation? When writing this book, there was a key question to be asked: was it a book about Christian communication or a Christian book about communication? If the former, then both its purview and its vocabulary would have been amended accordingly. If the latter, then its aim was to promote best practice, motivated by Christian conviction but expressed without Christian jargon. When you are writing, it doesn't matter what purpose you choose, but your words and style must serve it. Any piece of writing with too many aims is almost certain to disappoint.

Register

Once you know who you are writing for and what you are writing for, it should be possible to set the tone, or register, of your piece. This might best be described as 'how it reads', and will affect everything from the words you choose to the sentence structure in which you put them together.

Vocabulary

While some vocabulary is dictated by your subject matter, and may need to include specific terminology, the rest is really up to you. If your intention is to inform, you will want language which is clear, concise and unambiguous. If your intention is to provoke and intrigue, then you shouldn't be afraid of more overtly poetic and evocative language. You may even want to introduce some ambiguity, just to make people think. Where you are setting out to persuade, you will need to choose the kind of vocabulary which sets out your argument with clarity and passion. You may even need to shock in order to get your point across.

Of course, there are many literary sources to which we could turn to demonstrate these principles. However, I have chosen to draw them here from the Bible, since it is the source to which I have devoted many years of study. Written over many hundreds of years in different languages and from different cultural settings, it has much to teach us in terms of written media.

The Book of Acts is a historical account of the early years of the Christian Church. Arguments about the theological significance of these events are left to other people. Instead, the author sets out to tell the ongoing story after Jesus' ascension. An excerpt follows from Acts 2:1–12.

> When the day of Pentecost came, they were all together in one place. Suddenly a sound like the blowing of a violent wind came from heaven and filled the whole house where they were sitting. They saw what seemed to be tongues of fire that separated and came to rest on each of them. All of them were filled with the Holy Spirit and began to speak in other tongues as the Spirit enabled them.
>
> Now there were staying in Jerusalem God-fearing Jews from every nation under heaven. When they heard this sound, a crowd came together in bewilderment, because each one heard their own language being spoken. Utterly amazed, they asked: 'Aren't all these who are speaking Galileans? Then how is it that each of us hears them in our native language? Parthians, Medes and Elamites; residents of Mesopotamia, Judea and Cappadocia, Pontus and Asia, Phrygia and Pamphylia, Egypt and the parts of Libya near Cyrene; visitors from Rome (both Jews and converts to Judaism); Cretans and Arabs – we hear them declaring the wonders of God in our own tongues!' Amazed and perplexed, they asked one another, 'What does this mean?'

Note the use of the word 'like'. Since the author's aim is to record rather than interpret, he notes only what this sounded *like*, rather than what it *was*. Note the list of nationalities of those present – it doesn't make for captivating reading, but it is important to set these events in their historical context. Note also the use of direct speech at the end of the passage. Once again, the author's intention is to record rather than to interpret.

In the Book of Isaiah (40:12–17), we are looking at a different kind of audience. The prophet is addressing a group of frightened and demotivated people whose world has been turned upside down. Living in exile, they are uncertain about whether they will ever see their homeland again, and even less certain whether they still matter to God:

> Who has measured the waters in the hollow of his hand,
> or with the breadth of his hand marked off the heavens?
> Who has held the dust of the earth in a basket,
> or weighed the mountains on the scales
> and the hills in a balance?
> Who can fathom the Spirit of the LORD,
> or instruct the LORD as his counselor?
> Whom did the LORD consult to enlighten him,
> and who taught him the right way?
> Who was it that taught him knowledge,
> or showed him the path of understanding?
> Surely the nations are like a drop in a bucket;
> they are regarded as dust on the scales;
> he weighs the islands as though they were fine dust.
> Lebanon is not sufficient for altar fires,
> nor its animals enough for burnt offerings.
> Before him all the nations are as nothing;
> they are regarded by him as worthless
> and less than nothing.

Note the use of questions. Isaiah is seeking to capture the imagination and lift the spirit here – so, he suggests possibilities rather than closing them off. His language is extreme and poetic, painting a picture of a God who cups the oceans in his hands or weighs the islands in his fingers. He exaggerates in order to make his point, so that the nations are seen as nothing *in comparison to* the greatness of God.

In the passage from the Letter to the Philippians (2:1–5) below, Paul is seeking to persuade the members of the church in Philippi to behave differently on account of their relationship with him and their faith in Christ:

> Therefore if you have any encouragement from being united with Christ, if any comfort from his love, if any common sharing in the Spirit, if any tenderness and compassion, then make my joy complete by being like-minded, having the same love, being one in spirit and of one mind. Do nothing out of selfish ambition or vain conceit. Rather, in humility value others above yourselves, not looking to your own interests but each of you to the interests of the others. In your relationships with one another, have the same mindset as Christ Jesus ...

Note the accumulation of four short, repetitive phrases in the first sentence. Paul is 'stacking up' his arguments in the hopes that his readers will cave under the weight of them. He does a similar thing with the repetition of the word 'one' in the second half of that sentence. Although the language, unlike Isaiah's, is straightforward, the persuasive force of this writing is considerable.

Grammar

Grammar may be something you hoped never to read about again after abandoning your exercise books from school. However, grammar is no more than an agreed convention on how to organise and communicate our thoughts. Simple things like punctuation help to ensure that everybody makes the same connections between the same set of words. Conventions of grammar can be bent to the reader's advantage, as we saw in Paul's exceptionally long sentence above. All too often, though, unusual grammar arises by accident rather than design. This is a shame, since it means that a well-worded, carefully written piece of text can lose all its impact at the last minute. A reader who is enervated or confused by your poor punctuation will not stop to admire your clever words. Like it or not, grammar matters.

Personality

When all the questions have been asked, the register has been chosen, the vocabulary has been selected and the grammar observed, one thing remains – to be you in print as you are you in the flesh. Writing which is devoid of personality is devoid of interest to the reader. In the end, your writing style will reflect your personality, which is what will make it interesting. One of my roles as a minister has been to serve as a part-time tutor in preaching at a theological college. I love teaching the subject, and feel honoured to mark the sermons and assignments which are sent to me. However, I have lost count of the number of times that I have read a thoroughly researched essay which rehearses all the arguments and shows great evidence of study but tells me nothing about the student. If my students ever compare notes, they will probably ask each other: 'did he write at the end of yours: "yes, but what do *you* think?"?' Whether you are writing about a project, propounding an argument, expanding the imagination or persuading somebody to vote for you, it is vital that your personality should find expression on the printed page.

2.7   Broadcast media

The first time I was ever on national radio, an old friend wrote to me and said that she was in the kitchen preparing vegetables for a large number of guests when I 'appeared' right there with her. Apart from the fact that I was a welcome distraction from peeling the potatoes, this also reveals one of the key benefits of radio – intimacy. Unlike televised media, radio creates an intimacy between the voice of the broadcaster and the ears of the listener in the kitchen, in the car, in the potting shed or even in the shower. Even though a prime-time radio programme may reach up to ten million people at once, it nonetheless creates the illusion of intimacy and makes each listener feel that the programme is being delivered personally to their radio. This is significantly different to the nature of television, which often trades on the idea of being part of a massive audience beyond the room where you are watching.

Since my first foray into radio as part of a live Sunday-morning service, my radio journey has taken a number of twists and turns. Urged on by a good friend, I applied to the BBC to contribute to the morning 'pause for thought' slots on their flagship programme. Not surprisingly, they were not prepared to risk such an inexperienced person on their biggest audience. Instead, I got in touch with their late-night show, which goes out to half a million shift-workers, students, truck-drivers and anybody else who is awake in the early hours. After that, I got involved in producing these two-minute 'pause for thoughts' on a breakfast show too, with an estimated audience of three to four million. The challenge of producing something relevant, ear-catching, light and stimulating in the space of two minutes for an unchurched audience is not one to be under-taken lightly.

Apart from an interview in French on Swiss television and a pre-recorded interview with jazz singer Helen Shapiro for cable TV, my broadcast experience has all been on radio, and therefore it is upon that that I shall base what follows.

Context

When I first signed up to record late-night slots for the BBC, I was bombarded with information. I had a sheet describing the overall feel of the programme into which my script would be inserted. The next sheet gave me fifteen bullet points about the average Radio 2 listener and five separate statistics about the things they watch and read. I then had another set of facts about the specific audience for the programme in which my slot would appear. This included average age, male–female ratio, likely occupations, and keywords to use. To this I then added my own research, listening to several programmes to get a feel for the programme itself, and copying down sample scripts from the radio which I read through again and again. I also tried to talk to listeners to find out what they thought of the programme.

When I travelled to Manchester with my first set of scripts, which the producer had approved, I sat down in the studio to record the first one. I seem to recall that it was a script about the image of God. After a first run-through in that tiny studio, the producer then put a recording of the previous night's show through the enormous speakers. There was a blast of pulsating rock music, followed by the presenter making some ribald comments about women's lingerie. 'Now,' said the producer, 'you've got to fit into that'. It was a salutary moment. In this particular radio environment, I am a guest and should fit in accordingly.

Respecting the context in broadcasting does not mean that you compromise your content, but it may well mean that you amend it. I have now worked with half a dozen different producers; but Janet, my first one, left a lasting impression on me. She had worked with many different kinds of broadcast, from quiz shows and documentaries to live worship services. In all that time, she had found that religious people, and ministers in particular, were the hardest to work with. The reason for this was that they were often so 'precious' about their material that they felt uncomfortable amending it in any way. It was as if they felt it were a sort of 'holy writ', and to tamper with it would be wrong. Rather than adapting for their context, they acted as if it should adapt to them.

Content

Having understood the context, the broadcaster's next job is to write worthwhile content. In this regard, the fact that the script is only 120 or 150 seconds long is irrelevant. Regardless of the length of time allocated, the content needs to be relevant, interesting, imaginative, accessible and of some spiritual worth. If any of these elements is missing, the broadcast will fall short and impact badly on the rest of the programme. However, in writing the script with these aims in mind, there are equal and opposite dangers of twee application and unconvincing informality to be avoided.

On one occasion, I was recording a script about prejudice, alluding to Christ's story about removing the plank from your own eye before tackling the speck in your brother's. In an attempt to squeeze such spiritual content into the context of rock music and knickers described above, I succumbed to temptation and phrased it as: 'don't take the speck out of your mate's eye unless you've got rid of the dirty great plank in your own'. Now, I could have called it a clever piece of intralingual translation or an exercise in contextualisation. My producer simply called it 'wrong'. 'Would you actually say that in real life?' she asked – to which the answer was a resounding 'no'. An artificial jokey informality which tries to soften an otherwise challenging piece is an insult to the audience.

Since starting on those radio scripts, I have developed something of an instinct for spotting an episode or event with scriptwriting potential. Early on, I was told that the best piece of advice for writing successful scripts was to 'watch and listen' to life all around me – which I have done. I now carry a notebook so that I can note down any episodes which strike me as funny or useable. The problem, though, is when it comes to drawing any kind of deeper lesson from those episodes. Simply tacking on a phrase such as 'so there's a lesson for all of us' simply won't do. There has to be a natural link between the story recounted and the spiritual observation made, or people simply won't listen again. Thankfully, it rarely comes to that, as my producers usually wield the red pen with great enthusiasm at the writing stage. This is because the quality of the overall programme, including my small contribution, is their responsibility. I am in the hands of professionals. However, many times it is only when the written script is spoken that its shortcomings become apparent. I soon learnt to take my own pen with me to every recording session, as I knew that no script would make it from computer to microphone unscathed.

Tone

Often, though, it's not just amended words that get scribbled on my scripts. If I look back at them now, I see not just scored-out and rephrased sentences, but all sorts of other marks and notations too. Sometimes there is a double-headed arrow between two sentences, indicating a significant pause. Other times there is an arrow bending upward, indicating that I should raise the pitch of my voice towards the end of a sentence, or a downward arrow indicating the opposite. Occasionally a word is underlined to ensure that I give it special emphasis. On other occasions, there might be a line down the margin next to a particular paragraph with a single word next to it, such as 'warm' or 'upbeat'. The quality of radio is all about tone. A good script can be undone by a poor tone, and even an average script can be elevated by a warm and interesting tone.

So, what is it exactly? Tone is a combination of many things. For a start, there is clear diction. Since radio listeners cannot look at the shape of your mouth to help them make out an indistinct word or sound, it must be clearly pronounced by you. There must also be a warmth to your voice. A cold tone which might be appropriate in the courtroom or the station announcer's booth will not go down well on the radio. Tone involves the timbre of the voice too – the way it rises and falls creates the soundscape of the programme itself. If the changes are too sharp and angular, it may put people off, but if they are too gentle it may send them to sleep. A path needs to be found between the two. The other thing to remember is that the tone must be the kind of voice you would use in a small space, such as a living room, and not the tone you might use in a vast hall big enough to accommodate the programme's audience.

Attraction

One of the reasons that tone is so important is in order to battle the broadcaster's greatest enemy – the 'off' switch. No-one is obliged to listen to you on the radio, and they are just one button away from parting company with you at any moment. Unlike a live audience, where they must at least risk embarrassment or awkwardness if they choose to sit filing their nails, or get up and walk out, none of this applies on the radio. With the greatest of ease, they can switch you off or swap you for somebody else without the least hesitation. This means that the broadcaster must not only understand the context, hone the content and shape the tone accordingly, but must also use every available means to win the audience. The fact that they are listening right now does not mean that you have won them. They are only won if they choose to listen again and again.

In order to win this particular battle, the broadcaster must observe all the lessons above about appropriate content and interesting tone. It means choosing not only which words to use, but also how to pronounce every single one of them. However flat the script appears on the two-dimensional page, it must be turned into a three-dimensional landscape on the airwaves – with peaks and troughs, light and shade to keep the listener engaged. This may mean reading it dozens of times to yourself before you get anywhere near the recording studio – but so be it.

Conciseness

You might have thought, with all these concerns about contextually appropriate and tonally attractive radio, that the best thing is to write a longer script in the hope that somewhere along the line you will hit the mark. In my own experience, that has not been possible. Because of the time restrictions imposed by my particular pre-recorded slot, I have a maximum of eight to ten seconds' tolerance either way on each script. No script can be any shorter than 110 seconds or any longer than 160 seconds. These kinds of restrictions certainly make you consider every single word carefully. Although I can estimate approximately how many words I need to fill 120 or 150 seconds, I still have to revise every script several times. It means I must make choices about which bits of the story will be richly described and which bits will be baldly mentioned.

This is probably the area where my radio work has had the biggest impact on my other communication skills. When I preach, I am free to take anywhere between fifteen and twenty-five minutes over what I say. Within that time, there may be some repetition, a little hesitation, and a good few 'ums' and 'ers'. None of these things is acceptable on the radio. Repetition in a short piece is downright boring, and 'ums' and 'ers' are a waste of precious seconds and will be removed in the final edit. I would like to think that this has not made me paranoid about what I say, but it has made me very careful about choosing my words in the pulpit. Do I really need to say that? Does point B really have anything to do with point A, and has the whole thing delivered what it promised in the introduction? When I first started recording radio talks, a very experienced broadcaster and preacher said to me that 'every preacher should be produced' – and now I understand what he meant. The disciplines it teaches about concise language, careful tone and audience awareness are invaluable to any communicator.

Loneliness

It is obvious from all that I have written that my radio journey so far has been a joy. It is, though, very hard work. It means I have to swallow my pride when a precious script is returned covered in corrections. I have had to learn to take a deep breath when the same phrase must be recorded four or five times just to get the tone right. I have occasionally listened to the finished product when it goes out and have winced at an ill-chosen word or a clumsy tone. Overall, though, it has been an enormous privilege.

However, before leaving this particular area of communication, there is one more point to be made. Radio broadcasting can be a very lonely way to communicate. In four years of broadcasting and nearly 100 scripts, the amount of feedback I have received has been minimal. Unless people choose to write in to the programme, and unless the producer has time or inclination to pass on their comments to you, you may hear nothing. Like preaching, teaching and pastoral care, which are all described earlier in Part 2 of this book, it is best undertaken by those with a sense of calling to do it. That sense of calling will keep you motivated when no-one tells you how it is going. It will keep you motivated, too, when your producer tells you *exactly* how it's going!

2.8   Social media

To write about social media is a bit like painting the Forth Rail Bridge – by the time you have finished, it is time to start all over again. In the time it will take to write this section, proof-read this book and have it typeset, printed, marketed and delivered, the social-media landscape will have changed all over again. This serves only to emphasise the enormous difference between print and digital media. Never has there been an area of human communication where the rate of change and growth is so enormous. Networks which started out as a means for students to stay in touch with each other (Facebook) or for employees of a particular company to exchange simple messages (Twitter) have now grown to gargantuan proportions. Facebook, for instance, now has more members than there are residents of the United States of America. Twitter users exchange short messages or 'tweets' at the rate of over 100 million per day.

So, what's all the fuss about? There are numerous reasons for the popularity of these different social-networking platforms. Above all, their appeal is that they allow people to connect with each other. With no regard for creed, ethnicity, distance or time zone, they allow people to connect with others across Planet Earth. Not only that, but also they encourage the kind of blended communication to which we have become accustomed. Most of these platforms allow for the ready integration of text, graphics, photos, video and even GPS information which reveals the exact location of those who are communicating.

The democratisation of access to this kind of communication has had enormous impact in the fields of politics, marketing and news-gathering. When British forces landed in the Falkland Islands in 1982, we were largely reliant on radio reporting of the events. When the Twin Towers in New York were destroyed in 2001, most of us learnt about it through TV footage and phone-calls to inform us. When London was attacked by a series of bombs in July 2007, news footage was principally supplied by the public at the scene direct from their mobile phones, complete with videos. Political unrest in Iran, Burma and elsewhere has been tweeted to the world from those out on the streets among the protesters. Meanwhile, there are politicians who find that people who would never write to them, and are unlikely to subscribe to e-mail updates from them, are nonetheless happy to connect with them via social media. Large companies are now devoting significant proportions of their advertising budgets to social media, as they recognise that interacting with their customers brings more revenue than just advertising at them. By using the connectivity afforded by social media, they forge the kind of relationship with their customers which leads to brand loyalty.

Platforms

To describe all the social-media platforms would instantly render this section dated. However, before beginning to outline some principles, here is a guide to the types of social media which are out there.

Networks

These vary from the school-age Bebo, through Myspace to the enormously popular Facebook and professional networks such as LinkedIn. In general, they work through two-way association. In other words, those who participate must obtain each other's permission before becoming connected to each other. They lend themselves to the nurture of longer-term professional or personal relationships.

Micro-blogging

The most popular example of this is Twitter, where messages of no more than 140 characters are exchanged. The association here is not two-way, so people can choose to follow others without seeking their permission. Search engines such as Google have now started logging the messages exchanged on these sites, so they can be searched by the world at large.

Blogging

'Blog' is short for 'weblog', and these first started out as an online diary available for all to see. Most blogs are accessible to the public, and many offer the facility to subscribe, so that sub-scribers are contacted by e-mail each time a new article or 'post' is added. They vary from personal diaries to professional discussion forums.

Ironically, perhaps, my own involvement with social media came about through a print medium. When I first started writing a column for the *Baptist Times*, I wanted to facilitate interaction with my readers. While they could, of course, write letters to the paper, I knew that in reality few would bother. So, I started a blog where the columns were reproduced – and my journey into social media began. Over time, the blog, *http://richardlittledale.wordpress.com*, widened beyond the newspaper columns and began to take in other matters related to preaching and communication. It has now been visited by thousands all over the world, and often attracts lively discussions among its readership.

As the blog started to grow, I was advised to embark on Twitter as a means to direct people to it. I did so with enormous scepticism, since I suspected that Twitter was the preserve of the vacuous celebrity where nothing more than nonsense was exchanged. I could not have been more wrong. What started as a simple means to direct people to my blog soon became something much wider. I began to connect not only with people in my specific field of preaching, but also with others in related fields. As the diagram overleaf shows, there were both shared expertise and different specialisations among these people. Now, on any one day, I receive messages from at least three continents on all sorts of matters relating to faith, communication, preaching and current affairs.

As I got more accustomed to what Twitter had to offer, another idea was born. I read about an initiative in America called *One Twitter One Book*, where people were encouraged to

Richard: Preaching and communication

Bex: Social media and
Biblical communication

James: Communication
and PR

Scott: Marketing and
social media

Justin: PR and
marketing

join a Twitter-based book group. Each week, a different chapter of the book was discussed, and the group soon grew to several thousand. In May 2010, I launched '@chatbible' – a Bible discussion group on Twitter. It now has several hundred followers, and has played a key role in online projects for Christmas, Easter and Lent.

The insights which follow below are drawn from the journey thus far, and I am sure that there are plenty more to come.

Content

There is a curious disconnect between the intimacy of sitting alone at your laptop or PC and the millions who can access your material on the Internet once you have published it. In a way, it can be like swinging your legs off the bed, only to discover that you are standing not on the carpet but on the home plate for a major-league baseball game! It is easy to forget this, especially in the warm and cosy world of the friends and contacts with whom you choose to connect via social media. Unless you have put specific security restrictions in place, then you can count on your contributions on these platforms being both public and permanent. You cannot rely on your neighbour not reading them, nor indeed on a future employer who might be the other side of the world not seeing them. This is a particular warning to those who have allowed a gulf to develop between their online and offline personalities.

In his encyclical for the World Day of Social Communications 2011, the Pope warned, for instance, against 'the risk of constructing a false image of oneself, which can become a form of self-indulgence'. Slick, user-friendly software means that you can swiftly create an alter-ego for your online presence which bears little or no relation to reality. The ease of doing this makes restraint in avoiding it all the more necessary. Some key points on content follow below.

Interesting

There are millions of posts, tweets and updates finding their way onto social media every day. What reason would anybody have to read yours? Of course, they might do it simply because they know you. If you want to attract a wider audience, though, your material has to be interesting. Use catchy titles for blog posts or updates. Use different media to make yours visually attractive. Don't expect too much from the reader – any blog post which spills over more than one computer screen will have to be exceptionally good to retain the reader's attention. Remember that the Internet as a medium with its 'clickability' encourages a short attention span, and you must work within it.

Honest

As well as what we have said about integrity between your online and offline personalities, there must also be an honesty about your sources. If your contributions on social media are inspired by someone else, then say so. If your particular take on what they have said is interesting enough, it will not detract in the least from what you have written to acknowledge the source of its inspiration. Where you quote directly, you should acknowledge the source; and visual material should always be properly attributed too. The nature of digital communication means that once your contribution is published it is almost impossible to prevent someone else from cutting and pasting it into their own work. While there is little you can do about that, you can at least make sure that you are not guilty of doing it to the content of others.

Fresh

Since material on these various platforms can be updated at the click of a button, there is nothing worse than allowing your online presence to slip further and further out of date. If I visit a blog for the first time and see that the last post was written over six months ago, I am unlikely to visit again. Keep your contributions fresh and up to date, even if that means keeping them brief. Of course, there is an inherent danger with this approach – namely that you may end up writing something for the sake of it when you really have nothing to say. For me, one secret to keeping things fresh online is not finessing them too much. If I write a blog post today which is a little ragged or unfinished, I would rather correct that by a better one tomorrow instead of rewriting today's. This is partly to keep it fresh, and partly to encourage the kind of dialogue I am looking for. My intention was always to provide a forum where preachers and other communicators could share successes, failures, hopes and challenges together. The best conversations, either in person or online, sometime arise when half-formed thoughts can be aired rather than fully rounded arguments. To date, this strategy seems to have worked, with my blog audience growing from a few hits per day at the beginning to over 1,000 per month.

Sociability

It may seem obvious, but social media is intended to be sociable. This means that the kinds of rules which you would apply to a real conversation apply here too. If I am talking to you, and you use every gap in the conversation to promote yourself, then I will pretty soon tire of the conversation. Of course, if you have content online to which you want to draw people's attention, you need to do so. After all, by alerting them to your latest blog post or update, you are not forcing them to read it. However, if you seem always to be doing this, then you may exhaust people's goodwill.

It is important to discipline yourself to visit other people's online material and to comment where you can. In the first instance, this ensures that you are feeding your mind by other people's insights and creativity. Furthermore, it exploits the social dimension of social media to the full. It is designed to encourage us to 'browse' each other's material, gleaning what we can. There is another benefit too. Social media is 'sticky', so that every time you comment on someone else's material, it leaves a 'trackback' to your own. The likelihood is that if you visit someone else's blog, they are likely to visit yours. This likelihood is further increased if you leave a comment.

Personally, I have tried to avoid participating in online marketing campaigns through micro-blogging. It is not unethical, but I feel that once my contacts see I am inserting raw marketing into the conversation, they will wonder when it is me and when it is the product talking. The other aspect of being sociable is to be decent. There is no place in social media for bad language, defamation or religious, racial or gender prejudice. These are no more acceptable in the digital space than they are in the street or the home. The fact that the content of micro-blogging platforms is ephemeral, and may be forgotten about tomorrow, in no way excuses this kind of content.

Vulnerability

When I first launched '@chatbible' on Twitter, I felt distinctly vulnerable about the whole thing. The idea was to invite any and all who wanted to participate in a discussion of the Bible to do so. Each week, I would suggest a particular passage of the Bible, pose a question or two about it, and then allow the discussion to grow on '@chatbible'. Owing to the restrictions of Twitter, each contribution could be no more than 140 characters long, which helped to focus the mind. As I wrote on my blog at the time, it felt like

> throwing the front room of your house open to the public and then cracking the door open every now and then to see who has taken you up on the offer. On the one hand they might be in there putting their feet on the furniture; but on the other hand there might be nobody there at all and you feel like your house is too dull. (17 May 2010)

In fact, the whole thing has grown hugely, as noted above, and has attracted people from many branches of the Christian faith and a good few beyond it. In the 'space' created on Twitter, they have felt able to air their views, stumble towards some kind of clarity, and overturn a few old certainties to see what is underneath.

Social media provides a space where arguments, views and opinions can be aired and exchanged freely. Deeply held convictions can be exposed to scrutiny as never before. Not only this, but also the disconnect described above can mean that people express their opinions with far more vehemence and far less restraint than they might do face to face. While I hesitate to say that 'nothing is sacred' on social media, there are times when it may seem that way. This means that if you wish to enter into it, you must do so without being too precious about your content. Some people will love it, others will politely skirt around it, and others will robustly and critically engage with it. Of course, they could do this last with a book too. However, it takes far more effort to find the address of a publisher and ask them to pass on your comments than it does to click the 'reply' button to an update or blog post. Christianity as a faith thrives under scrutiny, I believe. Ever since Jesus told his disciples to 'let their light shine before men' (Matthew 5:16), Christians have been encouraged to live their lives in the fresh air of open debate. Some, though, may find the social-media landscape to be a more open space than they had expected.

Ethics

As yet, the ethics of social media is relatively unexplored territory. There is a growing unwritten code about etiquette, centred around the way we connect with each other or disconnect from each other. This also affects things like how and when we pass on other people's material. These are shallow, procedural things, though. We need a reasoned ethical debate to start thinking about deeper issues associated with these platforms. What are the ethical considerations associated with creating an online persona for myself? To what extent is true human interaction possible when I restrict my involvement on account of fears about identity theft? Not only this, but does my ability to connect with a person in desperate need in real time make me more morally responsible than I might have been when that news was mediated through another source? These are deep issues, but if we are to maximise the opportunities for truly human connection through social media, then they will have to be tackled. What follows is simply a note of some of the key questions which will need to be aired in any debate on the ethical future of social media.

Personality

Since social media allows me to create a personality for myself online, right down to the physical appearance which I present to others, this begs a question. What relationship should that virtual personality bear to my real one? After all, it is necessarily different to the real 'me', since my virtual self can be in several places at once. We might argue that there are good reasons for separating our real and virtual selves in order to preserve our private identity. How does that sit, though, with the kind of integrity demanded by the Christian faith? Writing in the first century, James stated that Christians should be known for their straightforward and integral talking: 'let your yes be yes and your no be no' (James 5:17). Should it be any different in the twenty-first century?

Connecting easily and connecting well

My online or virtual personality may be connected with many other people in cultures I have never visited and places I have not seen. At the click of a button, I can share my life and thoughts with them and they with me. However, we should not be fooled into thinking that easy connection is good connection. When I am connecting with those other people, am I really taking them seriously as human beings? Am I giving myself to those virtual encounters with all the heart and soul which I would give to an embodied one? We have all played the game of sounding like we are giving our undivided attention on the phone while actually doing something else. Social media just makes this easier to do.

Knowledge and responsibility

One of the great assets of social media is that it allows us to find out about what is going on around the world without the necessary filter of broadcast journalism. People on the streets in a political protest, or sheltering on the roof of their house from rising floodwaters, can update me in real time as to what is going on. It is both personal and immediate. Does this make me somehow more responsible for acting upon it, though? Of course, if I choose not to, the other 'virtual' person will never know – but that is not really the point.

When I first started my Bible discussion group on Twitter, I wrote an article entitled 'what would Jesus tweet?' Perhaps the more important question is 'how would Jesus tweet?'

Part 3
Making progress

3.1   Has communication happened?

For several years, it was my privilege to teach annually in a Bible college in Serbia. I taught with the help of a patient translator and soon learned to adjust to the rhythm of speaking through another person. Whenever a joke was told, there was a 'ripple' effect as it was understood first by those who grasped the English, and then by those who were waiting for the translation. Occasionally there was no laughter even after the translation, as humour is more culturally bound than we like to admit. Certain humour doesn't translate even if the words do.

One year, teaching through a particularly thorny section of the New Testament, I issued the class with two laminated cards. One bore the word *zasto?* (meaning 'why?') and the other the message *pa sta?* (meaning 'so what?'). The class were invited to raise them at any moment when they felt unclear about what was being said or why it mattered. In the event, they hardly ever did so – either because the teaching was clear or because they were polite. It is far more likely to have been the latter.

Perhaps we should issue people with credit-card-sized versions in English whenever we speak. After all, as communicators, surely we want to ensure that the message is getting across? Furthermore, as we saw in the section above, it is not just a case of *me* getting *my* message across. Unless communication is genuinely two-way, then we simply exist side by side, like silent tomes on a bookshelf gathering dust, or like two radios on a shelf, blaring out different programmes at the same time. If language is half as precious as we have suggested above, we dare not simply drop it and walk away when the going gets tough. The thing is, though, how do we quantify our gut feeling that the communication just isn't working?

Signs of failure

Body language

The first thing that most communicators will look for in order to judge whether it is working is the body language of those with whom they are communicating. The signs they must read are as diverse as the people who make them. Repetitive fiddling or fidgeting would be one particularly glaring example. Arms tightly folded may denote aggression, and resentment towards both the communicator and the message communicated. One leg balanced on top of the other and joggling up and down may be intended to convey nonchalance, but the communicator may see evidence of complete disengagement with what is being said. A person who seems absorbed in removing an imaginary piece of fluff from their sleeve is probably less than captivated by what they are hearing. Equally, the crossing and uncrossing of arms and legs is often an indicator that they are uncomfortable and have been sitting in the same place or position too long. While this may be attributed to the seating or the temperature and air flow in the room, it is probably wiser for the communicator to note it as well.

Eye movement

In a one-to-one context, there is a real problem if the person to whom you are speaking will not meet your eyes. This might be because they resent what you are saying, because they find it uninteresting, or because they fear your ability to read them. In a larger setting, people's eyes constantly flitting towards the clock or the exit door is a pretty good indicator that they would rather be elsewhere. The insights of neuro-linguistic programming may be of further help to us here, as they draw our attention to micro-gestures such as eye movement. Eyes up and towards the left may indicate that someone is thinking back to a previous memory rather than listening to what is being said now. Equally, if you notice the eyes looking up and towards the right, the person may be planning something for the future while pretending to listen to you. Of course, in many meetings today, all participants have portable computers open in front of them, ostensibly for taking notes. However, if you see their eyes rapidly scanning to and fro as if reading text, they are probably communicating with somebody else while claiming to listen to you. If they smile or laugh when you haven't said anything funny, there's a good chance that their friend on Facebook or Messenger has!

Need for repetition

As a communicator, there may be many reasons why you choose to repeat things. You may elect to do so to express your message in different ways in order to connect with both left-brain and right-brain people, for instance. You may choose to repeat the same message couched in different terms simply for the sake of emphasis and later retention. However, if your audience starts to ask you to repeat things on several occasions, it is likely that you are not communicating well. On the simplest level, this might be because they cannot hear you. Even if they can hear you, it may be that you are talking too quickly or too softly to make it easy to attune to your words. Alternatively, your vocabulary may be too complex or specialised for your particular audience. If this is the case, you may experience many interruptions to seek the clarification of particular terms, sometimes for the same word. On a deeper level, it may be that the things you say are failing to grab their attention, and as such are not retained. If their expectations of the meeting were different to yours, they will constantly be asking for a restatement of your objectives, either overtly or through many small details.

Unchanged behaviour

Often, the success of communication can only be measured over the long term. If one particular talk, sermon or presentation has gone well, this is clearly a cause for some celebration. However, the real value of the message communicated will be measured over the long term. Do people seem more motivated or informed or energised by the message they receive? In their powerful book *The Elements of Persuasion*, Maxwell and Dickman measure the value of stories by their power to transform. Whether or not we are using story, most communicators would wish to see their communication affecting the individual, and in turn that individual's immediate environment. If there is no discernible difference in behaviour or outlook over time, then it is a safe bet that the communication has failed to find its mark.

Evidence of success

Facial expression

Whether in a large gathering or a one-to-one context, the 'face recognition software' which is part of the human psyche means that we can soon read from others' faces whether or not communication is working. It might be that we see a light in the eyes as understanding dawns. Alternatively, we may note an animation to the facial features, a creasing round the eyes as a smile spreads, or a furrow of the brow as they listen hard. Even a sceptical raised eyebrow suggesting that the listener does not agree with our argument or accept our facts is evidence that they are engaged with what is going on. These and other micro-gestures of the face tell us that the person is truly participating in the communication. The enlivening of their faces means that they are willing to join in the dance of communication which animates the space between us.

Interaction

Occasionally, a preacher or other communicator will confess to me that they feel very threatened by others asking questions. They should not. In fact, people asking questions is evidence that they are engaging with the message they are hearing. To ask the speaker is to prove that they have concern for the subject and trust in the person of whom they ask the question. Not only this, but when they move on from questions to comments, where they frame the things they have learnt and heard in their own vocabulary and applied to their own situation, then something truly wonderful has happened.

On one of my lecturing trips to Serbia, I spent nearly two weeks lecturing through the dense theology and complex arguments of Paul's first letter to the Corinthians. It was hard work for both lecturer and listeners. However, when we concluded the lecture series by the class writing a letter together in response to Paul's epistle, the result brought tears to my eyes. Its mixture of humour, profound insight and warmth was evidence that they had truly absorbed the lessons of Paul's letter and made them their own. In most of the places where I communicate, I see it as a relay race. As a speaker or preacher, I pass the baton on to those who will hear. They take that baton, grasp it tightly in their hand and run on to the next chapter in their lives.

As a preacher, I am acutely aware of this. The sermon makes its first journey from my mouth to their ears. However, by far the more important journey is the one it makes from Sunday to Monday, when it interacts with the reality of daily life.

Changed behaviour

As much as unmodified behaviour may be evidence of failed communication, so changed behaviour may be evidence that we have got it right. This does not have to be in a spiritual sense either. If we have led a successful cookery demonstration, then the evidence of our successful communication will be the food which people go on to cook. The proof of the pudding will be in the eating, so to speak. If we have conducted a successful pastoral conversation and pointed people to resources beyond and above themselves, then the evidence of our success will be the strength with which they handle their situation. So often, communication is about empowerment. We may be empowering the other person by giving them information or motivation. We may be empowering them by enabling them to ask the right questions. However we do it, communication which empowers others to change themselves and then to shape their circumstances must be of the highest value.

When we take an honest look at how we communicate over the long term, we may be forced to conclude that things are not going as well as they might. Our aspirations and preparations are failing to yield the kind of results we were looking for. If this is the case, then it is time to act.

3.2 When it all goes wrong

In her excellent book *Adults Learning*, Jenny Rogers flips a well-known maxim on its head, saying that 'It is often said we learn by our mistakes. I have often thought how thoroughly misleading this statement is. It would seem truer to say that we learn by our successes as long as we know why we are being successful' (p. 62).

This is a wonderfully positive way to see things, and should contribute to a positive learning lifestyle. Rogers goes on to talk about feedback as a 'gift' which we give to each other. Let's be honest, though – feedback sometimes feels more like a kick in the teeth than a gift. People rarely speak up about your successes, especially when you are a communicator. Maybe this is why some people are so afraid of speaking in public, and list it as their greatest single fear apart from dying itself. When it comes to communication in public, people are far more likely to tell you when you have got it wrong than when you have got it right – that's just human nature.

So, let's suppose that you have laboured hard and long over your presentation. You have learnt from your peers, studied your books, assessed the needs of your audience and done every bit of homework you could possibly imagine. On the day, you have effortlessly combined research with repartee and insight with wit, or so you think. And yet, long before the 'happy sheets' (feedback forms) come back at the end of the session, you know it has all gone wrong. The glances at the clock, the shuffling of feet and the dull expressions communicate an eloquent story all of their own, and it's not the one you wanted to hear. What now? Before you plunge off into some abyss of self-inflicted despair and look for a new job, there are some worthwhile points to bear in mind.

Not the only one

You are not the first, and nor will you be the last in history, to discover that their finely honed piece of rhetoric has nothing like the impact for which they were hoping. Even a smooth communicator like John F. Kennedy, with his effortless charm and stirring speeches, was not above the occasional goof. When he gave his rousing speech on 26 June 1963 at the Berlin Wall, he inadvertently suggested that he was a kind of doughnut (a 'Berliner'). Despite paying tribute to his translator's skills in the very next sentence of his speech, the error had already been made.

In the Monty Python film *Life of Brian*, the only time that Jesus ever actually appears and speaks is in the distance at his famous Sermon on the Mount. Far off, at the back of the crowd, two men mishear his statement about 'blessed are the peacemakers' and assume instead that he is talking about 'cheesemakers'. On account of this misapprehension, a fight breaks out between them over the relative merits of cheesemaking as a trade. This is especially unfortunate given the nature of the subject matter. Of course it is nonsense, but it illustrates how even the most profound words are open to mis-interpretation.

We see this exemplified time and time again in the life and ministry of Jesus. Despite his crystal-clear teaching, there are plenty of people – from the religious authorities to his own family – more than capable of missing his point. His family often fail to understand him, and on one occasion he is accused by the religious leaders of working in league with Satan (Matthew 12:24). Hardly a resounding success on the communications front! Even his stalwart supporter, Peter, spectacularly misunderstands him, which is why he finds Jesus' description of his forthcoming suffering so unacceptable. All the clues Jesus had already dropped about the self-giving and sacrificial nature of his messianic mission had clearly failed to find their mark with Peter. In John's Gospel, Philip similarly misses the point when he asks Jesus to show the father to the disciples. Although the text does not allow us to hear it, I suspect there was a sigh in his voice as Jesus replied: 'Don't you know me, Philip, even after I have been among you such a long time? Anyone who has seen me has seen the Father' (John 14:9).

After the resurrection of Christ, we see the trend continue with the preaching of the early Church. Despite a resolutely Christ-centred Gospel message, the apostolic preaching is often perceived as something else. In the city of Lystra, Paul and Barnabas find themselves identified as the Greek gods Hermes and Zeus, and have to dissuade the crowd from sacrificing to them (Acts 14:13). In Ephesus, Paul finds himself at the centre of a dispute by the allied unions of silversmiths and idol-makers about the impact of Jesus-worship on their trade (Acts 19). None of this was intentional.

To know that these things happen is not an invitation to simply shrug our shoulders and not bother. However, it should be a reassurance that the human element in communication means that it will always be an inexact science. If we mess up in the pursuit of communicative excellence, we shall not be alone.

Doomed from the start

Some communication is doomed from the outset before either mouths or ears are opened. Sadly, this is often the case with industrial or religious disputes, where both sides come to the table so utterly convinced of their views that any form of genuine exchange is impossible. When such attitudes are brought to the communication act, no amount of brilliant speech or careful research can bridge the gap. Indeed, it is not so much a gap as a fortified frontier where none but the bravest will attempt to cross – and they are liable to perish in the attempt.

Communications may be doomed, too, when the expectations of each party, though genuine and positive, are entirely different. If person A thinks they are expecting one thing from a meeting, and person B thinks they are delivering another, there is likely to be frustration all round. This is the fault not so much of the communication itself as of the groundwork which precedes it. This may come about through advertising which is misleading or clumsy. A sermon which offers to 'solve the problem of suffering' is almost certain to disappoint, and a one-hour seminar which guarantees success at your next annual appraisal is setting itself up for a fall. Talking of annual appraisals, a perfectly innocent offer from your boss to 'chat about how things are going' may feel like a real threat if you think they are going badly. A glitch in expectations between the two parties involved in communication is sometimes all it takes to make it founder.

Look at the illustration opposite. Brian is frustrated because his message to Robert simply isn't bringing about the results he was hoping for. All those high aspirations about motivation and understanding which had fuelled him as he prepared for the meeting are now dashed by Robert's puzzled response. Robert, on the other hand, is puzzled because he doesn't really know what Brian is looking for. The gap between Brian's intention and his impact may well be caused by unrealistic or unclear expectations about the meeting before it first began. It may only be a short line in the picture, but it can make a big difference.

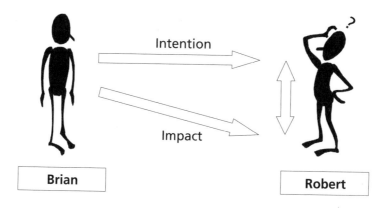

Not speaking, but listening

Poor old Brian may be entirely to blame for the failure of his communication. It takes two to tango, so to speak. Sometimes, the fact that a message has not been heard does not mean that it has not been spoken. A substantial piece of research was commissioned regarding the quality and content of preaching in churches in the United Kingdom. The conclusion, published in a report entitled *Imagine how the UK can be won* (Evangelical Alliance, June 2003), was that many of the finest 'teaching' churches were not addressing the workplace or daily life in their preaching. This conclusion was drawn on the basis of surveys filled in by congregations. The fact that sermons on the workplace have not been heard does not mean that they have not been preached. Far from it; people may have been dis-inclined or unable to hear the things said about their working lives, even though it *was* said. In my own ministry, I try not to preach specifically on the workplace, since that would instantly exclude the youngest, the oldest and the unemployed. How-ever, I make it my aim in every sermon to evince principles of Christian living which could be readily applied in home, college or workplace. If people have not heard your message, it may be because they were not listening to it!

So ...

It may be that you have looked at your most recent attempt at communication, and you feel you have covered all the angles above. You have been as clear as possible about your expectations. You have gone into it with realistic expectations. You have spoken for all you are worth, and they have listened for all they are worth, but the message simply hasn't got through. If this is the case, then it may be time for a change of technique.

3.3 Venturing into the discomfort zone

I enjoy acting, and always have done. A string of school plays in my early years turned into many happy miles of touring with a student theatre company – and it still surfaces once in a while in the pulpit. However, that said, there is acting and acting. When I spent a year in Belgium, I joined the local theatre school in order to work on my skills. Being asked to portray an entire scene using only one French word in different tones was certainly pushing the boundaries of my skill – both linguistic and theatrical! When it came to creating an entire believable character simply from the waist down by the way I walked, I knew I was in trouble! That said, it undoubtedly pushed me to discover new levels of skill in areas which I would never have investigated otherwise.

If you are committed to the communications enterprise, then surely you are committed to discovering and honing new skills wherever appropriate?

Beginner's lack

Of course, the usual phrase is 'beginner's luck' – and that is something most of us have experienced, whether trying out a new recipe, a new card trick or a new sport for the first time. However, there is also a considerable element of beginner's *lack*. In other words, when I first begin to try a new technique, I will inevitably make mistakes. I will be less proficient and competent than others who have tried it before me, and will feel stupid by comparison. I will lack what they appear to have in abundance. And yet, without this initial fallow period, I can never aspire to be where they are or to do what they do.

When I first began writing scripts for radio broadcast, it seemed like every one was going to die the death of a thousand edits. Even after the scripts had zipped to and fro between the producer and myself, I still didn't have the finished article in my hand. Sitting in the studio, headphones clamped on head, I would listen as the producer told me patiently and carefully what should be changed and how it should be said. If I wanted to 'play the game', I needed to heed her warnings. After all, she knew more about the programme's half-million listeners than I did, and I was in the hands of an expert. I pretty soon learnt to take a pen with me to every recording and expect to use it. There are one or two of my scripts now where it is hard to pick out the original typing because it has disappeared under a storm of scribbled comments, arrows and amendments. As a beginner in a new field, I have a lack, both of skill and experience. Both can be compensated for, but I must be prepared to swallow my pride in order to do so.

Ask the right questions

If we are going to push ourselves beyond the boundaries of communication which have always been familiar to us, we need to ask ourselves some basic questions. The following can be helpful examples:

1. Am I an analytical person – fascinated by facts and figures, and frustrated by the absence of precision?
2. Am I a reflective person, energised by contemplation and solitude?
3. Am I a natural raconteur, making sense of everything by seeing its place in a wider narrative?
4. Am I an active person, enlivened by activity and frustrated by 'just' thinking?

While these questions have a wide bearing on our overall character, they can have a specific impact on how we communicate too. Those who try to communicate in ways unsympathetic to their natural character frequently come unstuck and produce disappointing results as a consequence. Often, the constraints passed on to us by our schooling in the past or by our working environment in the present oblige us to ignore these natural inclinations – to the detriment of all.

Of course, it can be difficult to answer these questions about ourselves. Habits over the years may have buried our natural communicative persona so deep down that it is hard to excavate it. Trusted friends can be a real help here. They can often tell us things about the way we come across to which we are entirely blind. If you are going to ask for these kinds of insights, though, it is worth crossing the work/leisure divide in order to do so. People whom you meet in the pub or at the sports club may be able to tell you things about your natural communication style of which your work colleagues would be utterly unaware. It works the other way, too. A confident communicator about 'business' matters can turn into a nervous wreck when communicating in another context. Friends from each 'side' of your life can help to complete the picture.

Technology can be of service here, too. Never turn down an opportunity to listen to or watch yourself if you can. This is in order not to encourage a kind of atavism, but to hone your skills. Cheap and simple digital technology means that it is not hard to obtain a recording of your presentation at work or your sermon in church which you can pore over afterwards. Listen out for warmth and accessibility of tone, as well as clarity of vocabulary and pace of delivery. If you are watching a video, look out for repetitious gestures or repeated touching of your face. Involuntary acts, such as shuffling from foot to foot or rattling loose change in your pocket, may never be commented on by anyone – but the camera will certainly pick them up. Thankfully, you will almost always be surprised by the bad *and* the good things you discover.

Check the options

Once you have made the decision to venture into uncharted communication territory, and have equipped yourself with some insights into the kind of person you are, the possibilities are endless. There are all kinds of different avenues you could pursue. An indication of some of them is given below.

Storytelling

This may be anything from retelling the classic fables of old in such a way as to illustrate your contemporary point, to writing your own entirely original fiction in order to get your message across. More and more businesses are acknowledging the power of story, and encourage managers and consultants to articulate the company's mission and challenges through this medium. A friend of mine is a senior management consultant, and we have often pored together over the need to create a narrative structure for even the driest of topics. It is expected of him, and many others in his profession, to have an overarching narrative to their presentation, which can then be expanded with details after the imagination of the client has been captured.

Technology

Those of us who have been fashioned in a communication school which relies utterly upon the power of the spoken word may resent the arrival of new technology in just the same way as we might resent the arrival of a brash and noisy next-door neighbour. Not only this, but also the linear nature of a PowerPoint presentation means that there is very little scope for altering it once that presentation has begun. What it gains in polish and panache it may lose in flexibility. However, new technology, with its ability to display clear points in an ordered and well-illustrated fashion, should not be readily dismissed. Communication Luddites beware!

Multi-media

This is really a branch of technological communication. However, it does not stop at the projection of still images and words to illustrate your point. It may combine speech with movie clips, sound bites and images in order to produce a potent message. A talk may be illustrated with live streaming video news, an audio bite of the latest hit song, or a webcam chat with a person on the other side of the world.

Fusion

This kind of communication may combine multi-media with the traditional tools of rhetoric and maybe even the odd bit of dramatisation or the use of real objects to illustrate a point. In a world of high-tech multi-media presentations, the use of a piece of fruit or a lump of coal to make a point can jolt an audience into taking notice of what is said. A friend of mine recalls with a wry smile the time he outsmarted all his colleagues in his high-tech environment by offering oranges on his stand instead of streaming video!

Interrogative

Although not for everyone, nor for every circumstance, there is a place for interrogative communication, especially in those contexts where people expect everything to be just one-way. The pleasant surprise of being asked to contribute in a context where your only expectation was to listen can sometimes release the best insights. The onus is on the communicator to phrase questions in such a way that they are both simple and open. Simple words like 'so?' and 'because' can yield all sorts of interesting results. Of course, the communicator has to be prepared that his or her questions may provoke many others from the hitherto passive audience; but that need not be a bad thing.

When reviewing which techniques are best to choose, it is worth remembering the adage that 'permanent change is here to stay'. The communications environment is evolving at a rapid rate as it keeps pace with changing technologies. Also, our own styles as communicating creatures change as we get older. Our preferences for the audio and the visual, the didactic and the interactive may change with the passage of time and circumstance. This should encourage us to try different styles without fear.

Anticipate the pitfalls

Watching a documentary about the training of Her Majesty's Household Cavalry, I winced, along with most of the TV audience, at the number of times one raw young recruit fell from his horse. He did it from sitting, from standing, backwards, forwards and every which way in between. The bruises were only to be imagined. However, when the interviewer commented on this, he simply stated that it was all part of the training, and that he had been led to expect such things.

If you try a new style of communication, there will be bumps and bruises along the way. For the first few times, it may well sit uncomfortably with both you and your audience. They will be discomfited, and you will be exhausted. Preparation time will be longer for you, and you may find people commenting far more on the style than on the content of what you have communicated. However, these are the bruises along the way, and they just have to be endured. In the end, like the cavalryman, you will be able to hold your head high and stay on the horse!

Communication has far more to fear from ossification than from innovation. Changing nothing is a far greater threat than changing something. To change something may alienate some people for some time. Changing nothing may alienate everybody in the long run.

3.4 Learning to communicate through community

Those best able to help in developing the self are
those comrades in adversity who also struggle to understand
themselves.

These are the words of Reg Revans, Olympic athlete, research scientist, National Coal Board and National Health Service manager, and Professor of Industrial Management. Revans learnt the value of co-operative learning, and the price we pay without it, from watching his father, who was one of the investigators into the 1912 *Titanic* disaster. After graduating, he worked initially in a research laboratory where the scientists pooled their knowledge and examined their challenges. This was done without recourse to any higher or external input, since they were the 'experts' in their field.

Later on, as a senior manager in the NCB and the NHS, he noted that both coal pits and hospitals worked better when they worked their way towards their own solutions to problems by pooling their collected expertise and experience, rather than looking for pre-packaged knowledge from outside. He also coined what has come to be known as Revans' Law: *for an organisation to survive, its rate of learning must be at least equal to the rate of change in its external environment.* Out of his research and insights, the techniques of action learning have been born.

Action learning

So, how does action learning work? A group of five or six people, all working in the same field or working environment, meet together regularly as a learning set. With a facilitator to help them, they go through the following steps at their meetings:

1. Members of the learning set have a given amount of time to 'bid' for their particular issue to be aired.

2. Once an issue-holder is chosen, they air their particular problem. In doing so, they may describe the people involved, the solutions previously tried and their feelings about it.

3. Other members then ask disciplined and focused questions, which avoid either an autobiographical element of 'this happened to me' or any value judgement.

4. The issue-holder then sits outside the learning set while the other members discuss and record their insights and suggestions.

5. The issue-holder then returns to the set and leads a discussion on the issue using the new insights provided.

In essence, it may seem like little more than the old adage 'a problem shared is a problem halved' writ large, but it has been found to have positive results. By encouraging those within a given field to learn from each other, rather than leaning on outside help, it fosters a learning environment which helps organisations to grow and adapt.

Action-learning alternatives

Many professional communicators would fight shy of the approach described above. After all, they are quite accustomed to being the external expert called in to help and therefore have no interest in doing themselves out of a job! All too often, a person who is used to standing before a silent audience – in a church, a classroom or a lecture theatre – is something of a prima donna and would find the idea of 'horizontal' learning unsettling at best.

However, surely those who are committed to excellence in communication should leave no stone unturned? It may well be worth the communicators themselves forming learning sets, where they could air their frustrations and triumphs about how their communication is going. In many ways, this might be at its most valuable if those sets were to comprise communicators from different fields. Thus, a set which had a couple of preachers, a teacher or two, a local newspaper journalist and a management consultant could yield very rich and fruitful discussion. Each member could return to their 'native habitat' stimulated by the surprising insights of others.

If this is not possible, then the formation of learning sets within a given environment could certainly be pursued. In churches, for instance, all those who provide the preaching might form a learning set where they could examine their triumphs and failures in the pulpit. In that context, they could not only share the issues but also pray for each other, from which great strength might be drawn. In schools, colleges and consultancies, similar learning sets could be established, albeit without the overtly spiritual element.

Barriers to communal learning

Since this may sound to some like a fanciful scheme, perhaps it is better to acknowledge the barriers at the outset.

Busy-ness

Many communicators are busy people in their field and elsewhere. The idea of taking time out 'just to' chat about how things are going seems too much to ask. It's not that they doubt its value to some people, just that they doubt its value to *them* in the midst of their hectic schedules. The sighs, slumped shoulders, clock-watching and knowing winks exchanged at the start of many a training session are evidence of this.

Arrogance

Sometimes it is not so much that people are busy, but that they are unconvinced of their need for any further training or input. These people are lone wolves, getting out there and delivering the goods on their own time after time. Why would they want to sit down with others and discuss how it's going? If they want to enhance their skill set, they would rather do it privately by reading or by engaging the services of a coach.

Fear

Oddly, the arrogance described above may in fact be a disguise for deep underlying fear. The longer you go on working entirely on your own, the greater the chance of someone else eclipsing you without you knowing about it. Attending a learning set might seem like an invitation to someone else to show you that you are inadequately prepared or out of date. Oddly, this would seem even worse from people in your own field than it would from those outside it. At least with those outside it you could dismiss their views as ignorant!

Habit

We are all creatures of habit, to a greater or lesser degree. Sometimes habit can be reassuring, like an old coat which slips on so easily because we have worn it into shape. The habits we have formed as communicators allow us to perform 'off the cuff' where necessary, relying on past experience to see us through. However, at other times, habit can be more of a straitjacket than a coat – restricting our movement and preventing us from exploring anywhere or anything new. We stick with what works well because we fear what might work better. Better the devil you know …

The parable of the talents

When I had already been preaching for over thirteen years, my attention was drawn to a new Masters course in preaching at one of London's theological colleges. My initial reaction was to ignore it entirely. After all, I knew how to preach already – and, as the old saying goes, 'if it ain't broke don't fix it'. It took a visit to one of Jesus' simplest and best-known parables to burst my bubble and reveal my pride for what it was. In Jesus' story, a departing nobleman issues money to each of three servants when he leaves for a foreign country (Matthew 25:14–30). On his return, each servant is held to account for what they had done with their portion of money, or 'talent'. Times without number, I had heard this story told as an object lesson for children, a reminder from Jesus himself to do our best. However, looking at it through adult eyes, I saw it as a divine injunction to treat a God-given talent with respect, and to ensure that He had some yield on his investment. To say that my preaching worked was no excuse not to improve it.

So, I embarked on a three-year degree programme in my spare time. Alongside others from different denominations, I studied and wrestled and honed my skills. Sometimes I had to stand up in front of a class of my peers and preach a sermon which they would deconstruct. For every module, I had to provide a 2,000-word commentary on my own sermon, explaining my rationale behind it and assessing its value. This was hard work, no doubt about it. To be called to account with intellectual rigour for something you have been doing every week twice a week for over thirteen years is no small thing. However, at the end of it, I like to think that the talent is in rather better shape than when it started.

A commitment to learning is incumbent upon all who teach or influence others. Even if it is a step into the unknown, the potential of learning about communication in groups definitely needs to be explored.

3.5   Just do it

I have to confess, I am not the world's biggest fan of country and Western music. Steel guitars and stetsons are not really my scene. However, there is a song written by Doug Crider and performed by Suzy Bogguss entitled 'Love goes without saying'. You don't need to know anything about the rest of the song to know that he has a point. Our fear of saying things wrong, or saying them inadequately, leads us not to say them at all. When we take that path, it is a short step from an awkward silence to an angry silence, and then to a silence so deep and entrenched that it cannot be broken. It's not that we decide to stop speaking to each other, more that we never decide to start. And so, love goes without saying . . .

Take the risk

We should not minimise the risks of opening your mouth and deciding to speak out anyway. After all, as soon as a word is written or spoken, it can never be undone. It can be retracted or apologised for, but once out of your mouth or off your pen it has a life of its own. In spoken words, you might say something foolish or inaccurate. You might unwittingly give voice to your innermost thoughts which should really have stayed private. In some contexts, you might start a minor war! Then again, in other contexts you might avert a major tragedy.

Though not minimising the risk, in the end failed communication is less of a risk than a failure to communicate at all. In marriages, in families, in international diplomacy and interfaith dialogue, the secret is to keep talking at any cost. Of course, this means that we will sometimes get it wrong. However, the price of not doing it at all is far higher.

Embrace your vulnerability

It is true, in many different fields of human endeavour, that our best is produced in the worst moment. Suffering, hardship, war and disaster have often led human beings to look deep down inside themselves and discover that their God-given abilities are greater than they ever imagined. If you embark on the adventure of communication with a full awareness of your vulnerability and your capacity for error, you may just find yourself pleasantly surprised by what ensues. A toddler's first haltingly formed word, or a lover's first attempt to declare their feelings, are made more precious, surely, by the vulnerability from which they emerge.

Enjoy your humanity

It is often said that to 'err is human', while forgiveness is God's prerogative. However, there can be such creativity in the erring. Many members of the animal kingdom have a capacity for invention. A monkey, for instance, can use its dextrous fingers to find a way into food that is locked away. Squirrels can defeat most squirrel-proof bird-feeders, given time and hunger to help them. So far as we know, though, only humans have the capacity to invent language in order to keep up with their ever-changing environment. As the technological and political landscape alters, so language is constantly morphing in order to make sense of it. Those whose work is to compile dictionaries will testify to this. To be part of this articulate, inventive and occasionally foolish human race is an inestimable privilege. When we blunder our way through the linguistic maze to get our message across, it is part of our unique capacity to be human. Mistakes be damned – the joy is in the trying!

Pass the soap!

With the linguistic backdrop changing all the time, language itself can never be pinned down by overly restrictive definitions. Attempts in France to resist the corruption of the French language by rejecting foreign imports such as 'le weekend' have foundered for exactly this reason. Language today is not the same as it was yesterday, and it will be different again tomorrow. It's not just that there are new words entering our vocabulary, either. Words such as 'gay' have undergone a radical transformation, and others such as 'spin' will do the same. Try to pin language down too tightly, and it is like grabbing a bar of wet soap – the harder you grip, the further it shoots out of your hand. It must be better to enjoy the communication for what it is, and – like a skilful surfer – to ride the wave of ever-changing language.

Luther's T-shirt

Martin Luther's writings are a strange mixture of the profound, the coarse, the simple and the incomprehensible. However, one of his more memorable phrases, as mentioned in section 1.2 above, is *peccator fortiter*.

It means 'sin boldly' and expresses Luther's belief that, as human beings, we should not live our lives in a state of perpetual fear of 'getting it wrong'. Instead, we should accept that we shall probably mess up, and continue bravely and hopefully anyway. This applies especially when we are communicating, as we have already seen.

In the college where I trained as a minister, I grew very familiar with the profile of this great Reformer. There was a stone bust of Martin Luther which used to move mysteriously around the college from room to room, on one occasion landing up on my desk in the very early hours of the morning! All this means that if Martin Luther were to come back, I would recognise him instantly. If he did, it would be my great pleasure to present him with a T-shirt, preferably in a nice loud colour, with the legend *peccator fortiter* on the front. I hope he would wear it. I think it would suit him.

If he wouldn't, though, I would gladly do so. I have stuck my neck out in order to provoke thought, discussion and reflection on this complex business of communication. Some of my words will intrigue, some will stimulate, and others will quite simply annoy. In writing it all, I have sought, if anything, to sin boldly.

Who needs words? We all do, since that's the way we were made. We need to use them, understand them, invent and reinvent them – and, in so doing, we shall make many mistakes and describe many new realities.

Read the book, wear the T-shirt, but for God's sake keep talking.

Acknowledgements

Every effort has been made to trace copyright-holders of works quoted in the text. We are grateful both to the publishers who did not require permission to be acknowledged, and to other publishers for permissions to reproduce the following material.

On p. 7, the information from Phil Baguley, *Successful Workplace Communication* (London: Hodder Education, 2009), © Phil Baguley, 2009, is reproduced by permission of Hodder Education.

On p. 2, the quotation from John Berger, *Ways of Seeing* (London: Penguin, 1972), © in all countries of the International Copyright Union by Penguin Books Ltd 1972, is reproduced by permission of Penguin Books Ltd. All rights reserved.

On pp. 20 and 24, the quotations from John P. Kotter and Dan S. Cohen, *The Heart of Change: Real-Life Stories of How People Change Their Organizations* (Harvard, MA: Harvard Business Press, 2002), © 2002 John P. Kotter and Deloitte Consulting LLC, is reproduced by permission of Harvard Business Publishing.

On pp. 31 and 33, the quotations from Peter Shaw, *Conversation Matters* (London: Continuum, 2005), © Peter Shaw, 2005, are reproduced by kind permission of Continuum International Publishing Group.

On pp.32–3, the quotation from Dana L. Strait et al., 'Musical experience and neural efficiency: effects of training on subcortical processing of vocal expressions of emotion', *European Journal of Neuroscience*, 29 (2009), pp. 661–8, is reproduced by permission of John Wiley & Sons.

On p. 37, the quotation from an interview with Walter Brueggemann is reproduced by permission of *Mainstream* magazine.

On p. 46, the quotation from Alexander Elchaninov, *Diary of a Russian Priest*, is reproduced by kind permission of Faber & Faber Ltd.

On p. 54, the quotation from Samuel Beckett, *All That Fall* (1965 edn), is reproduced by kind permission of Faber & Faber Ltd.

On p. 78, the quotation from William Maltby cited in *The Preacher*, no. 130 (July 2008), p. 30, is reproduced by permission of the College of Preachers.

On p. 121, the quotation from Jenny Rogers, *Adults Learning* (London: McGraw-Hill/Open University Press, 2007), © Jenny Rogers, 2007, is reproduced with the kind permission of Open University Press. All rights reserved.

Bibliography

Works cited in the text are included here alongside suggestions for further reading.

Books

Baguley, Phil, *Successful Workplace Communication* (London: Hodder Education, 2009).

Berger, John, *Ways of Seeing* (London: Penguin, 1972).

Bolinger, Dwight, *Language: The Loaded Weapon* (Harlow: Longman, 1980).

Browning, Guy, *Office Politics* (London: Ebury Press, 2006).

Brueggemann, Walter, *Finally Comes the Poet: Daring Speech for Proclamation* (Minneapolis, MN: Fortress Press, 1989).

Byron Jones, Kirk, *The Jazz of Preaching* (Nashville, TN: Abingdon Press, 2004).

Cooling, Margaret, *Creating a Learning Church* (Oxford: BRF, 2005).

Edwards, Betty, *Drawing with the Right Side of the Brain* (London: HarperCollins, 2008).

Elchaninov, Alexander, *Diary of a Russian Priest* (London: Faber & Faber, 1967).

Flemming, Dean E., *Contextualization in the New Testament: Patterns for Theology and Mission* (Leicester: IVP, 2005).

Harrisville, R. A. and Walter Sundberg, *The Bible in Modern Culture* (Grand Rapids, MI: Eerdmans, 2002).

Hayes, Philip, *NLP Coaching* (London: McGraw Hill/Open University Press, 2006).

Kotter, John P. and Dan S. Cohen, *The Heart of Change: Real-Life Stories of How People Change Their Organizations* (Harvard, MA: Harvard Business School Press, 2002).

Lischer, Richard, *The End of Words* (Grand Rapids, MI: Eerdmans, 2005).

Maxwell, Richard and Robert Dickman, *The Elements of Persuasion* (New York: Collins, 2007).

Mitchell, Jolyon, *Visually Speaking* (Louisville, KY: Westminster John Knox Press, 1999).

Nouwen, Henri, *Reaching Out* (London: Collins Fount, 1982).

Obama, Barack, *Dreams from My Father* (Edinburgh: Canongate, 2007).

Rogers, Jenny, *Adults Learning* (London: McGraw-Hill/Open University Press, 2007).

Sanneh, Lamin, *Translating the Message: The Missionary Impact on Culture* (New York: Orbis, 1990).

Shaw, Peter, *Conversation Matters* (London: Continuum, 2005).

Thistleton, Andrew, *New Horizons in Hermeneutics* (London: HarperCollins, 1992).

Tubbs Tisdale, Leonora, *Preaching as Local Theology and Folk Art* (Minneapolis, MN: Augsburg Fortress, 1997).

Willimon, William, *Peculiar Speech: Preaching to the Baptized* (Grand Rapids, MI: Eerdmans, 1992).

Articles

Appleyard, Bryan, 'A guide to the 100 best blogs – part 1', *Sunday Times* (15 February 2009).

Burns, Barbara Helen, *Contextualization in the New Testament*: review, *Connections*, 7:3 (2008), pp. 40–2.

Chiang, Samuel E., 'Oral communications and the Gospel', *Connection*, 8:2 (2009), p. 34.

Morgan, Nick, 'How to become an authentic speaker', *Harvard Business Review* (November 2008), pp. 1–5.

Paul, Ian, 'Poetry as preaching', *The Preacher*, 130 (July 2008), pp. 5–6.

Strait, Dana L., Erika Skoe, Nina Kraus and Richard Ashley, 'Musical experience and neural efficiency: effects of training on subcortical processing of vocal expressions of emotion', *European Journal of Neuroscience*, 29 (2009), pp. 661–8.

Webliography

Benedict XVI, *Truth, Proclamation and Authenticity of Life in the Digital Age: Message ... for the 45th World Communications Day*, 24 January 2011 (see www.vatican.va).

Cartner-Morley, Jess, 'Life at snail's pace', www.guardian.co.uk/lifeandstyle/2009

www.actionlearningassociates.co.uk/regrevans.html

www.filmsite.org/butc.html

www.managementfutures.co.uk